1001 HOMONYMS AND THEIR MEANINGS

A Dictionary Of Homonyms With Defining Sentences

By Raymond E. Laurita

LEONARDO PRESS
Camden, ME

Copyright   LEONARDO PRESS   1992
PO BOX 1326
Camden, Maine 04843

All rights reserved. No part of *1001 HOMONYMS AND THEIR MEANINGS - A Dictionary Of Homonyms With Defining Sentences* may be reproduced or transmitted in any form or by any means, electronic or mechanical, including photocopy, recording, or any information retrieval system, without permission in writing from the company.

Printed in the UNITED STATES OF AMERICA.

ISBN 0-914051-29-6

To my wonderful, loving brother Dick, who has given all who have known him a legacy of memories filled with friendship, kindness, generosity, courage, and decency.

REL

1001 HOMONYMS AND THEIR MEANINGS

Contents

Introduction	....	xi
Guide To Using 1001 Homonyms and Their Meanings	....	xiii

I - The Long Vowel Sound of A
1. a-e	ape, same, care	....	1
2. ai	aid, ail, air	....	8
3. ay	bay, May, play	....	10
4. ei	sleigh, eight	....	12
5. ea	great, pear	....	12
6. ey	they, prey	....	12
7. e-e	there, where	....	13
8. ae	tael, Gael	....	13
9. au	gauge	....	13
10. a	bass	....	13
11. ee	nee	....	13

II - The Short Vowel Sound of A
1. a	add, flag, tap	....	14
2. au	laugh	....	20
3. ai	plaid	....	20

III - The Long Vowel Sound of E
1. ee	eel, see, feet	....	21
2. ea	ear, eat, tea	....	28
3. e-e	cede, gene	....	31

v

4. ie	field, piece	....	32
5. ei	Neil, seize	....	32
6. e	be, me, we	....	33
7. i-e	pique	....	33
8. i	chic	....	33

IV - The Sort Vowel Sound of E
1. e	edge, leg, ten	....	34
2. ea	bread, tread	....	36

V - The Long Vowel Sound of I
1. i-e	ice, fine, hide	....	37
2. i	I, fight, high	....	42
3. y-e	rhyme, thyme	....	44
4. ie	die, lie, tie	....	44
5. ye	lye, rye	....	45
6. y	by, fly	....	45
7. ei	height, sleight	....	46
8. uy	buy, guy	....	46
9. oi	choir	....	46
10. eye	eye	....	46
11. aye	aye	....	46

VI - The Short Vowel Sound of I
1. i	in, it, slip	....	47
2. y	cyst, myth	....	53
3. i-e	give, live	....	53

VII - The Long Vowel Sound of O
1. o-e	cone, hole	....	54
2. o	cold, so	....	59
3. oa	oak, boat	....	61

4. oe	doe, toe	....	62
5. ow	bowl, tow	....	64
6. ou	dough, soul	....	64
7. oh	oh	....	65
8. ew	sew	....	65
9. owe	owe	....	65
10. eau	eau	....	65

VIII - The Short Vowel Sound of O
1. o	odd, stop	....	65
2. a	watt, what	....	68

IX - The Long Vowel Sound of U
1. u-e	use, mule	....	69
2. ue	cue, hue	....	69
3. ew	yew	....	70
4. ewe	ewe	....	70
5. ueue	queue	....	70
6. you	you	....	70

X - The Short Vowel Sound of U
1. u	rug, stub, us	....	71
2. o-e	come, some	....	74
3. o	son, ton, won	....	74
4. ou	rough, tough	....	75

XI - The Long Diphthong Sound of U
1. oo	boot, too	....	75
2. ew	brew, threw	....	79
3. u-e	lute, ruse	....	81
4. ou	roux, through	....	81

5. ue	blue, rue	....	82
6. ui	bruise, cruise	....	82
7. u	flu, gnu	....	83
8. o	do, two	....	83
9. oe	shoe	....	83
10. eu	rheum	....	83
11. ieu	lieu	....	83

XII - The Short Diphthong Sound of U
1. oo	book, foot	....	84
2. ou	would	....	84

XIII - The Diphthong Sound of AU
1. au	haul, taught	....	85
2. a	all, bald	....	86
3. aw	law, dawn	....	87
4. ou	ought	....	87

XIV - The Diphthong Sound of OI
1. oi	boil, oil	....	88
2. oy	boy, toy	....	89
3. uoy	buoy	....	89

XV - The Diphthong Sound of OU
1. ou	loud, out	....	90
2. ow	cow, sow	....	90

XVI - The r-Controlled Sound of AR
1. ar	art, far, hard	....	92
2. ear	heart	....	93

XVIIA - The r-Controlled Sound of OR
1. or   or, fort   94
2. oar   boar, hoarse   95
3. ore   core, sore   97
4. our   four, mourn   97
5. ar   quart, quartz   98
6. oor   door   98
7. orr   torr   98

XVIIB - The r-Controlled Sound of OR
1. or   word, world   99

XVIII - The r-Controlled Sound of ER
1. er   herd, tern   100
2. ear   earn, pearl   101
3. ere   were   102
4. ier   tierce   102

XIX - The r-Controlled Sound of IR
1. ir   birth, sir   103

XX - The r-Controlled Sound
             of UR ....
1. ur   fur, hurt   105

Appendix A
The Alphabetical Homonym Index 107
    (Includes total number of homonyms
        for each letter of the alphabet)
Appendix B
The Polysyllabic Homonym Index
    (Complex Roots) 123

Appendix C
The Quantitative Homonym Index
    (Simple Roots) 133

Appendix D
    A - Definitions 135
    B - Abbreviations 137

Bibliography 138

Introduction

The decision to write a book, any book, is an awesome undertaking, for once begun, it takes on a life of its own. As its pages begin to fill, it becomes ever more demanding. It nags and pulls and begs for more and more attention to fill out its missing parts. Being the husband of a wife who has borne our six offspring, I wouldn't dare to compare it to the nine month period of gestation during which a growing human being makes the same kinds of demands, but in an abstract, perhaps even spiritual sense, the two experiences do have much in common.

From the moment the idea for a book about homonyms first entered my consciousness as a fleeting series of neuronal cell firings a number of years ago, I have known that it would have to become a completed reality. Precisely how the material encompassed in such an effort would be researched and organized, so it could become a useful tool for users from every stratum of the intellectual continuum of spellers, was problematical, right up to the point when the final copy was being readied to go to press. But it had to be done. I had to make my own personal effort to fill, at least as I perceived it, a need and write the "definitive homonym book." Who among us has not hesitated, at least for a brief instant, and posed the question - *Is it sheer or shear, faint or feint, rain or rein or reign?*

Most competent spellers eventually achieve a high degree of mastery of words which have the same sound but different spellings, meanings, and origins. However, a lifetime of teaching students of all kinds, among them many brilliant individuals who could simply not master these sound-alikes, leads me to believe there will be many who will appreciate the material in these pages.

The organizational system used to present the more than 1001 homonyms (over 1300), should result in success for most who seek to discover the correct word for their individual purposes. It is organized with a cross referencing system, one made possible by representing the entire body of homonyms comprising the book in two ways: first, in terms of the specific individual vowel sound which serves as the basis of each homonym, and second, through a full alphabetical indexing of the entire list of homonyms.

Of one thing I am sure. The next time I am asked by a teacher, or a parent, or a member of the audience at one of my lectures, about how to help a student find the correct spelling of *meat or meet, or son or sun,* I will not have to rely on the kind of direction teachers have given from time immemorial to, *Go and look it up in the dictionary,* advice which leaves much to be desired. Rather I will have an answer at the ready... and, a handy resource available for use. And now, so will you.

Guide To Using This Dictionary

What are homonyms?

Although dictionaries define the term *homonym* in several different ways, the meaning used in this book is that *a homonym is a word which agrees with another in pronunciation, but differs from it in meaning, origin, and spelling.**

* Some dictionaries use the words *homonym* and *homophone* synonymously, and some classify words with different meanings but the same spellings as also being *homonyms or homophones.* In these pages, only words which have *the same sound,* **but different spellings,** are presented as being *homonyms,* a view suggested as being most useful by WEBSTERS NEW TWENTIETH CENTURY DICTIONARY, and others. In a recent discussion, my friend Richard Lederer indicated that he, along with many others, preferred the word *homophone,* an opinion which is perfectly legitimate and acceptable.

How are the homonyms organized and presented?

Each of the homonyms in this book is presented in two ways:

A - As part of an overall category based on the specific sound carried by the root vowel element, *no matter how that vowel is spelled.*

In this dictionary, all of the homonyms are organized within the confines of 20 different general sound categories. Each of these groupings is then further subdivided into the various possible vowel spellings able to be discovered after a prolonged search.

For example, homonyms containing different spellings are presented for words containing the long vowel sound for a, as it is heard in *take, say, pain, reign, great, they, etc.*

I - The Long Vowel Sound of A

Alphabetic Representation	Sound-symbol Representation	Number of Homonyms
1. a-e	ape, same, care	62
2. ai	aid, ail, air	49
3. ay	bay, May, play	24
4. ei	sleigh, eight	18
5. ea	great, pear	8
6. ey	they, prey	8
7. e-e	there, where	4
8. ae	tael, Gael	2
9. au	gauge	1
10. a	bass	1
11. ee	nee	1

Total - 171 Homonyms

Homonyms containing each of these specific sound-symbol spelling categories are then presented as follows:

1. a-e (ape, ale, same)

   ale -   *We drank ale in the old pub.*
   Also: *ail - I ail from a bad cold.*

ate - irregular past tense form of *to eat* - *Last night we ate by candlelight.*
Also: *eight* - *Are you eight or nine years old?*

2. ai (aid, ail, air)

aid - *The doctor came to my aid.* or *Can I aid you in solving your problems?*
Also: *aide* - *General Washington sent for his aide to ask his advice.* or *The girl made an excellent nurse's aide.*
aide* - See *aid*   (2.ai - p.8)*
ail - See *ale*   (1.a-e - p.1)*

* Each sound category is a separate entity and references to other spelling forms are made **within the specific category**. If a reference is to be made outside the category, it is indicated clearly, as in the following:

6. ou   (dough, soul)

course - See *coarse* XVIIA   (2. oar - p.96)
dough - See *doe*   (4.oe - p.62)
four -   See *fore* XVIIA   (3. ore - p.97)

As is demonstrated above in the homonym correlates *ale-ail* and *aid-aide*, related spellings are always presented together as an aid for those who are uncertain about associated original spellings.

Since it is rarely the definition of these small root words which causes difficulty, each is defined through the use of *defining sentences*, those in which context serves clearly to indicate which spelling form is associated with a desired meaning.

Grammatic information is also present in a general way in these defining sentences, and more specifically in Appendix A. When a word has a single grammatic function, context serves to convey its usage as a noun, verb, adjective, adverb, preposition, etc. However, when a word has two, or even more, different meaning or grammatic possibilities, the form followed in the *defining sentences* is to present, first, *noun* usage, second, *verb* usage, and third, *adjective, adverb,* or other usage. In any event, as with all word usage, the final designator of grammatic function is context. Every effort has been made to use sentences which are as contextually clear and meaningful as is possible as aids in determining grammatic function.

The second method used to represent homonyms is as follows:

B - As part of the **Alphabetical Homonym Index.** (Appendix A)

In this appendix, the entire list of homonyms comprising this dictionary is presented in alphabetical order, along with the page where it appears with its pronunciation correlate, and the grammatic uses which are presented in the defining sentences. The uses of this appendix are many and varied and should prove invaluable for both poor spellers, and for instructors engaged in the task of helping them to better understand the organizational structure underlying our print system. Of interest also to serious investigators are the quantifications accompanying each letter of the alphabet. For example, several letters, such as s and w, have more than one hundred homonyms listed, while others, such as u and z, have only one.

Do some homonyms become homonyms because they have more than one pronunciation?

Yes, but all of the pronunciations found in this dictionary are acceptable in one or more of the references used in amassing these lists. When a pronunciation is presented that is not the *most* common, it is either accompanied by a superscript to indicate this fact, or by other means to insure clarity. The homonyms *waft-waffed* will serve to demonstrate this process:

> **waft** [2] - *I felt a waft of fresh air.* or *The scent of roses will waft through the night air.*
> Also: **waffed** - Scottish and British Regional - past tense form of *to waff* - *The flag waffed in the breeze.*

In this example, the most common vowel pronunciation for *waft* is that associated with the vowel **a** in *father*. But the second most commonly used form allows *waft*[2] to rhyme with *haft* or *raft.*.

Another example of this process can be observed in the homonyms *kill-kiln:*

kill - *The hunter shot the deer and got his kill.*
>or *A creek or stream is sometimes called a kill, especially in place names, as in Wallkill.* or *The object of the war seems to be only to kill the enemy.*

Also: *kiln* [1] - *A kiln is an oven used to process materials for burning and hardening, such as grain or clay.* or *He used the new oven to kiln the bricks.* (In kiln[2] the final consonant **n** is pronounced)

What is contained in the Appendices?

The appendices in this book contain the following information:

Appendix A - *The Alphabetical Homonym Index (Simple Roots)*
This section contains a complete alphabetical listing of every homonym involving a *simple root* in the dictionary.(See Appendix D for the definition of *simple root*) Each entry contains a quantification indicating the number of homonyns initiated by each consonant, information about grammatic function,* and the specific page where each homonym appears:

<u>C</u> (102 homonyms)
cache	(n-v)	p.15
Cain	(n)	p. 8
calk	(n-v)	p.87

* Since this work is not an attempt to duplicate existing dictionaries but rather to make the search for homonyms less cumbersome, every possible word meaning is not included. However, a serious attempt has been made to include the most commonly used meanings whenever possible. By using this book, those who need further information will at least have the proper spelling to use in aiding them in their search.

Appendix B - *The Polysyllabic Homonym Index (Complex Roots)*

This section contains a complete listing of homonyms which involve polysyllables, such as, *cannon-canon, disgust-discussed, weather-whether*, etc. Because of the complex structure of these word forms, they comprise a far more limited portion of the total number of homonyms found in the language, almost certainly less then 25% of the overall total:

discreet - *His behavior was very* **discreet**.
discrete - *A* **discrete** *thing is one which is distinct.*
disgust - *The ugliness of the place filled me with* **disgust**.
discussed - *Tom and I* **discussed** *the whole situation.*
docile - *The* **docile** *tiger was submissive.* (See **dossal**)*
* Most homonyn pairs are presented in sequence. When this isn't possible because alphabetization interferes, the reader is directed to the associated homonym, as in the case of *docile-dossal*.

Appendix C - *The Quantitative Homonym Index For Simple Roots*

Most homonyms consist of words comprised of simple base roots, either in isolation (*bale-bail, time-thyme, ware-where, etc.*), or in combination with an inflection (*mist-missed, seize-seas, wild-wiled-whiled, etc.*). The total quantification of these homonyms is presented, both for the 20 sound categories individually, for these categories as a totality, and for the combined totality for both simple and complex roots.

IX	The Long Vowel Sound of U	11
X	The Short Vowel Sound of U	38
XI	The Long Diphthong Sound of OO (boot)	82

Appendix D - *Definitions and Abbreviations*

Although there is a limited number of terms requiring definition, those that are necessary for clarification are defined as simply and as clearly as possible.

I - The Long Vowel Sound of A

Alphabetic Representation	Sound-symbol Representation	Number of Homonyms
1. a-e	ape, same, care	62
2. ai	aid, ail, air	49
3. ay	bay, May, play	24
4. ei	sleigh, eight	18
5. ea	great, pear	8
6. ey	they, prey	8
7. e-e	there, where	4
8. ae	tael, Gael	2
9. au	gauge	1
10. a	bass	1
11. ee	nee	1

Total - 171 Homonyms

1. a-e (ape, ale, same)

ale - We drank **ale** in the old pub.
Also: **ail** - I **ail** from a bad cold.
ate - irregular past tense form of to eat - Last night we **ate** by candlelight.
Also: **eight** - Are you **eight** or nine years old?
bade - irregular past tense form of to bid - I **bade** you good night.
Also: **bayed**- past tense form of to bay - The dog **bayed** at the moon.
bale - Did you unload the **bale** of cotton yet? or Are the men going to **bale** the rags now?
Also: **bail** - The judge set a high **bail**. or Bill is in jail and I'm going to **bail** him out. or She used a cup to **bail** the water from the small boat.

bare - *The carpenter is going to bare the old beam to see what it looked like originally.* or *The closet was bare.* or *The spy laid bare all the secret treaties.*
  Also: **bear** - *The huge brown bear attacked the man.*
base - *Is that building resting on a solid base?* or *The vessel returned to its base.* or *The runner forgot to step on third base and he was called out.* or *The general is going to base his troops on the hill.*
  Also: **bass** - *The tone he played was a bass.* or *The choir needed a good bass.*
based* - See **baste** (1.a-e - p.2)
baste - *Before sewing the coat, the semstress will baste the material.* or *The cook will baste the meat by pouring pan drippings over it.*
  Also: **based** - the past tense form of *to base* - *The judge based his verdict on the evidence.*
bate - *The cold made me bate* (lessen the force of)*my breath.* or *The man tried to make the falcon bate* (flap wildly) *its wings.*
  Also: **bait** - *What kind of bait did you use to catch that big fish?* or *Can the small boy bait his hook?*
brake - *The brake on the car was off.* or *The man tried to brake the car to a stop.*
  Also: **break** - *I gave him a break because he was so young.* or *Did you break the window?*
cane - *The old man walks with a cane.* or *The old man is going to cane the chair and make it like new.*
  Also: **Cain** - *Cain was the brother of Abel.*
chased* - See **chaste** (1.a-e - p.2)
chaste - *The young people lived chaste and pure lives.*
  Also: **chased** -past tense form of *to chase* - *The policeman chased the young man down the street.*
Dane - *A Dane is a native of Denmark.* or *My name is Dane.*
  Also: **deign** - *She didn't deign to answer his insult.*
daze - *After the fall, the man was in a daze for a week.* or *A blow to the head will often daze a person.*
  Also: **days** - the plural form of *day* - *We will arrive in two days.*

fare - *The fare on the bus was ten cents.* or *How did he fare with his new project.*
  Also: **fair** - *We went on the rides at the fair.* or *The girl had fair skin.* or *The man didn't play fair.*
faze - *The bad weather didn't faze the ship's captain.*
  Also: **phase** - *The class completed the first phase of the project on time.*
flare - *They shot a flare into the air and the men in the boat saw it.* or *She didn't let her temper flare up.*
  Also: **flair** - *The child had a natural flair for music.*
gage - *I gave my word as my gage that I would repay my loan.*
  Also: **gauge** - *The gauge on the furnace was broken.* or *Bill can gauge character very well.*
gale - *The gale winds blew down the barn.*
  Also: **Gail** - *Is her name Gail?*
  Also: **Gael** - *A Gael is a Gaelic-speaking Celt of Scotland, Ireland, or the Isle of Man.*
gate - *They built a new gate in the old fence.*
  Also: **gait** - *Both the man and the horse had an unusual gait as they walked around the ring.*
glare - *The teacher had a penetrating glare.* or *Why does he like to glare at people?*
  Also: **glair** - *Glair is raw egg white used in glazing or sizing.* or *The painter wants to glair the walls.*
grate - *Dad shook the grate and the ashes fell through it..*
  Also: **great** - *The students thought their teacher was a great person.*
graze - *The cows like to graze in that field.* or *Did you graze his arm as you passed by?*
  Also: **grays** - *the plural form of gray* - *The artist used several grays in his painting.*
hale - *The man wants to hale me into court for no reason.* or *He looks hale and hearty.*
  Also: **hail** - *I saw some hail fall that was as big as golf balls.* or *Did they hail him as their leader?* or *Where does he hail from?* or *He stood in the road trying to hail a taxi.* or *Hail to the king!*
hare - *A hare is much like a rabbit.*
  Also: **hair** - *The bald man had lost all of his hair.*

3

haze - *There was a dull haze over the city this morning.* or *The club will haze the new members.*
    Also: *hays* - present tense form of *to hay* - *The man hays the field slowly.*
knave - *The crafty knave stole all the horses.*
    Also: *nave* - *The nave is a central parts of a church.*
lade - *The men can lade the boat with cargo now.*
    Also: *laid* - irregular past tense form of *to lay* - *Last week Mom laid the baby in its crib.* or *The hen laid an egg last night.*
lane - *His house was on an old country lane.*
    Also: *lain* - irregular past participle of *to lie* (to rest) - *I had just lain down when the siren rang.*
laze - *It's fun to just laze around on hot days.*
    Also: *lays* - plural form of *lay* - *The church choir sang two lays.* or *She lays her child in the crib.*
made - irregular past tense form *to make* - *I made a cake.*
    Also: *maid* - *She is a house maid.*
male - *The person in the picture is a male, not a female.*
    Also: *mail* - *They went to pick up the mail.* or *Did you mail the letter yet?*
mane - *The lion had a beautiful mane.*
    Also: *main* - *We walked down the main street.*
maze - *The cave explorers said that the cave was like an intricate maze.*
    Also: *maize* - *Maize is a grain native to the new world.* or *The color of her dress was maize* (orange yellow).
nave -   See *knave*   (1.a-e - p.4)
paced* - See *paste*   (1.a-e - p.5)
pale - *His face was pale.*
    Also: *The farmer carried a pail of milk to the barn.*
pane -   *The pane of glass is broken.*
    Also: *pain* - *She felt a sudden pain in her arm.* or *It will pain me to hurt you.*
pare -   *I can pare the apple with the new peeler.*
    Also: *pair* - *Dad bought a new pair of shoes.* or *The teacher will pair the children by size.*
    Also: *pear* - *I ate a juicy pear under the pear tree.*

paste - *The papers were held together with sticky paste.* or *Why did you paste these things to the wall?*
  Also: *paced* -the past tense form of *to pace* - *The man paced back and forth in the waiting room.*
phase - See faze   (1.a-e - p.3)
phrase - *That sentence has an interesting phrase in it.* or *Jody tried to phrase her sentence properly.*
  Also: *fraise* - *A fraise is a defensive barrier made of pointed stakes or barbed wire; it was also the name applied to a type of neck ruff in the 16th century.*
  Also: *frays* - the plural form of *fray* - *The team played in many heated frays.* or present tense form of *to fray* - *His collar frays because he wears it every day.*
place - *We vacationed in a very nice place.* or *I lost my place in line.* or *I am going to place your name on this list.*
  Also: *plaice* - *Plaice is an edible marine flatfish.*
plane - *The plane rose rapidly after take-off.* or *The carpenter used the plane to shave some wood from the board.*
  Also: *plain* - *It was a plain ordinary old box.* or *The cattle graze on the plain.*
plate - *The cook served the meat on a hot plate.* or *The metal worker is going to plate my silver for me.*
  Also: *plait* - *The child was wearing a long plait* (braid) *down her back.* or *The girl will plait her hair into braids.*
rale - Although it is not the most common pronunciation, it is acceptable to pronounce this word as though it rhymed with *rail*. It is defined as *an abnormal respiratory sound, one usually indicative of underlying pathology.*
  Also: *rail* - *The new train travels on only one rail.* or *A rail is a small marsh bird which is not well adapted for flying.* or *The farmer is going to rail the pasture.* or *The student stood before his class to rail about injustice.*

raze - The bulldozer will *raze* the old mill and level the ground in a single day.
   Also: *raise* - The doctor told me to *raise* my arms.
   Also: *rays* - the plural form of *ray* - The sun's *rays* were very strong today.
sale - All these things are on *sale*.
   Also: *sail* - We went for a *sail* in our new sailboat. or Do you like to *sail* in the morning?
shake - I gave the can a good *shake* to mix the contents. or Tom would like to *shake* your hand.
   Also: *sheik* [2] - A *sheik* is a Moslem religious official, or a leader in an Arab family ir tribe.
   See also *sheik* [1] III (6.ei - p.33)
spade - I dug a deep hole with my new *spade*. or A *spade* is a black symbol that appears on one of the four suits of playing cards.
   Also: *spayed* - past tense form of *to spay* - The vet *spayed* the cat to make it infertile.
stake - I hammered a *stake* into the ground. or He gave me a *stake* (money) to get my business started. or The man walked over his land to *stake* it off accurately. or The bank is going to *stake* me to a loan.
   Also: *steak* - He ate the *steak* rare.
stare - The artist gave his painting a long, hard *stare*. or Why did he *stare* at the picture for so long?
   Also: *stair* - The baby could not reach the first *stair*.
tale - The *tale* he told wasn't true.
   Also: *tail* - That dog has a short *tail*. or He is going to *tail* his kite again. or Why did you *tail* (follow) that car so closely?
   Also: *tael* - A *tael* is a unit of weight in eastern Asia.
tare - The *tare* is a weedy plant that grows in a grain field. or The *tare* is the weight of a container which is deducted to obtain the net weight of a package.
   Also: *tear* - Mom had a long *tear* in her new dress. or I had to *tear* my coat to get it off the hook.
vale - My farm is located in a *vale*.
   Also: *vail* - (Archaic) He had to *vail* (doff) his hat.
   Also: *veil* - She wore a heavy *veil*.

vane - The weather **vane** shows the wind is from the west.
  Also: **vain** - All his efforts were in **vain**. or He is very **vain** about his appearance.
  Also: **vein** - The blood poured from the cut in his **vein**. or This coal is from a **vein** in the old mine.
wade - See **weighed** (4.ei - p.12)
wale - The cloth had a wide rib or **wale**.
  Also: **wail** - Did you hear that baby **wail**? or The baby will **wail** loudly if you don't feed it soon.
  Also: See **whale** (1.a-e - p.7)
wane - The storm began to **wane** at about nine.
  Also: **wain** - The farmer put the bales of hay in his **wain**.
  Also: **Wayne** - **Wayne** is my friend.
ware - This word refers to articles of the same kind and is usually used in combination with a word indicating the material, or type of material, with which the article is identified, as in *glassware, earthenware, software, hardware*, etc.
  Also: **wear** - Mom gave her old coat heavy **wear**. or You must **wear** warm clothes in winter.
  Also: **Where** did you leave the car keys?
  (Properly pronounced *hwere*. See **whale**)
waste - There is a great deal of **waste** when Dad cooks. or It's a sin to **waste** food when people are starving.
  Also: **waist** - The slim woman in the picture had a red belt around her tiny **waist**.
wave - A huge **wave** washed over the beach. or Why did the small child **wave** to us as we passed him by?
  Also: **waive** - I will not **waive** my claim to the inheritance.
whale - The huge **whale** swam freely. (Although the digraph **wh** is properly pronounced as **hw**, as in **whale** (*hwale*), many people, of all educational backgrounds pronounce it as though it began with the simple individual sound for **w**.
  See **wale** (1.a-e - p.7)
* A root with an inflection

2. ai (aid, ail, air)

aid - *The doctor came to my aid.* or *Can I aid you in solving your problems?*
    Also: *aide* - *General Washington sent for his aide to ask his advice.* or *The girl made an excellent nurse's aide.*
aide* - See *aid*   (2.ai - p.8)
ail -   See *ale*   (1.a-e - p.1)
air - *We stood in the clear fresh air and breathed it.* or *Mom is going to air out the room.*
    Also: *heir* - *When his father died, the boy was the only surviving heir.*
    Also: *ere* (Archaic) *I shall return early next year ere (before) spring comes.*
bail - See *bale*   (1.a-e - p.1)
bait - See *bate*   (1.a-e - p.2)
braid - *The girl's hair was in a braid.* or *Will you teach me how to braid my hair?*
    Also: past tense form of *to bray* - *A donkey brayed.*
braise - *The cook said to braise the meat well.*
    Also: present tense form of *to bray* - *The donkey brays when I put on its harness.*
Cain - See *cane*   (1.a-e - p.2)
fail - *Did he fail the test again?*
    Also *faille* - *Faille is a woven fabric.*
faille - See *fail*   (2.ai - p.8)
fain - See *feign*   (4.ei - p.12)
faint - *I fell down in a faint.* or *I am going to faint.*
    Also: *feint* - *The general began the battle with a feint toward the enemy's strongest point.* or *Why did the boxer feint with his left hand and then use his right?*
fair -   See *fare*   (1.a-e - p.3)
flair - See *flare*   (1.a-e - p.3)
fraise - See *phrase* (1.a-e - p.5)
Gail -   See *gale*   (1.a-e - p.3)
gait -   See *gate*   (1.a-e - p.3)
glair - See *glare*   (1.a-e - p.3)
hail -   See *hale*   (1.a-e - p.3)

hair -   See *hare*   (1.a-e - p.3)
laid -   See *lade*   (1.a-e - p.4)
lain -   See *lane*   (1.a-e - p.4)
maid -   See *made*   (1.a-e - p.4)
mail -   See *male*   (1.a-e - p.4)
main -   See *mane*   (1.a-e - p.4)
maize   See *maze*   (1.a-e - p.4)
pail -   See *pale*   (1.a-e - p.4)
pain -   See *pane*   (1.a-e - p.4)
pair -   See *pare*   (1.a-e - p.4)
plaice   See *place* (1.a-e - p.5)
plain - See *plane* (1.a-e - p.5)
plait - See *plate* (1.a-e - p.5)
praise - The speaker heaped *praise* on the class for their good work. or I want to *praise* the class for their good work.
   Also: *prays* - present tense form of *to pray* - The small child *prays* by her bedside.
rail -   See *rale*   (1.a-e - p.5)
rain -   I like to stand in the *rain* and get soaking wet. or Dad said it's going to *rain* today.
   Also: *reign* - The king had a long *reign*. or The queen wants to *reign* justly over her people.
   Also: *rein* - A *rein* is a strip of leather attached to a bridle to control an animal.
raise - See *raze*   (1.a-e - p.6)
sail -   See *sale*   (1.a-e - p.6)
staid - He is a very *staid* and solid person.
   Also: *stayed* - past tense form of *to stay* - Dad and I *stayed* in the barn that night.
stair - See *stare* (1.a-e - p.6)
straight - See *strait* (2.ai - p.9)
strait - A *strait* is a narrow passage of water joining two larger bodies of water.
   Also: *straight* - The road was *straiught*. or The flying arrow went *straight* to its target.
tail -   See *tale*   (1.a-e - p.6)
vail -   See *vale*   (1.a-e - p.6)
vain -   See *vane*   (1.a-e - p.7)
wail -   See *wale*   (1.a-e - p.7)

wain - See *wane* (1.a-e - p.7)
waist - See *waste* (1.a-e - p.7)
wait - The girls had a long *wait* for the plane.
  or We had to *wait* for a full ten minutes.
  Also: *weight* - The *weight* of the box
  was fifty pounds.
waive - See *wave* (1.a-e - p.7)

3. ay (bay, May, play)

bay - Jack went swimming in the *bay*. or They sat in the
  bay window. or Did the wolf *bay* at the moon?
  or The *bay* colt was more red than brown.
  Also *bey* - A title of respect in Turkey.
bayed* - See *bade*   (1.a-e - p.1)
brayed* - See *braid* (2.ai - p.8)
brays* - See *braise* (2.ai - p.8)
cay - A *cay* is a small islet made of coral or sand.
  Also: *Kay* - Sir *Kay* was the foster brother of King
  Arthur in the legend. or *Kay* is a nickname for
  Katherine.
days* - See *daze*   (1.a-e - p.2)
fay - A fairy or elf is sometimes called a *fay*. or Did the
  builder *fay* the beams together tightly?
  Also: *fey* - The *fey* child appeared to be enchanted,
  as if under a spell. or Everyone thought the *fey*
  woman was clairvoyant.
frays* - See *phrase* (1.a-e - p.5)
gray - He drove away in a *gray* car.
  Also: *grey* - variant spelling of *gray*.
grays* - See *graze*   (1.a-e - p.3)
hay - The men loaded the *hay* onto the wagon. or The farmer went to *hay* his fields.
  Also: *hey* - an interjection used to show surprise or
  wonder - *Hey!* That's very nice!
  Also: *heigh* (Archaic) - *Heigh*, I need help! (Also
  pronounced as *high*, as in *heigh*-ho)
hays* - See *haze*   (1.a-e - p. 4)
Kay -   See *cay*   (3.ay - p.10)

lay - *The choir sang an old lay at the service.* or *My uncle is a lay (of the laity and not ordained) preacher in the church.* or *Lay the child on its bed carefully.* or *The hen cannot lay any more eggs.* or *We have to lay low for now.*
   Also: *lei* - *When the plane landed in Hawaii, they put a lei (woven chain of flowers) around my neck to welcome me.*
   Also: *ley* - variant spelling of **lea** and used in poetry to mean *grassland or meadow.* (Also pronounced to rhyme with **lee**)
lays* - See *laze*   (1.a-e - p. 4)
nay - *He didn't like the new law so he voted nay.*
   Also: *neigh* - *The horse gave a mighty neigh and the noise frightened us.* or *The old horse likes to neigh when he is hungry.*
   Also: *nee*[1] - derived from French and used to identify a married woman's maiden name, as in *Mrs. Mary Jones, nee Smith.* (nee[2] is a second pronunciation and acts as a homonyn for **knee** - III [1.ee] p.23)
pray - *Do you kneel down to pray?*
   Also: *prey* - *The owl is a bird of prey and hunts for mice at night.*
prays* - See *praise*   (2.ai - p. 9)
rays* - See *raise*   (2.ai - p. 9)
slay - *Why did Cain slay Abel in the Garden of Eden?*
   Also: *sleigh* - *The old horse pulled the sleigh over the snow.* or *We are going to sleigh on the hill.*
spayed* - See *spade*   (1.a-e - p. 6)
swayed* - See *suede*   (7.e-e - p.13)
tray - *She put the dishes on a large tray.*
   Also: *trey* - *A card or a die with three pips, or marks, on it is a called a trey. It also means three (3).*
way - *Which way did the car go?*
   Also: *weigh* - *How much did the box weigh?*
   Also: *whey* - *Little Miss Muffet, sat on a tuffet, eating her curds and whey.* **Whey** is the watery part of milk that separates from the curds.
* A root with an inflection

4. ei (sleigh, eight)

deign -	See *Dane*	(1. a-e - p. 2)
eight -	See *ate*	(1. a-e - p. 1)
feign -	He tried to *feign* (pretend) *sleep*.	

Also: *fain* - (Archaic) *He was fain* (ready) *to fight.*

feint -	See *faint*	(2. ai - p. 8
heigh -	See *hay*	(3. ay - p.10)
heir -	See *air*	(2. ai - p. 8)
lei -	See *lay*	(3. ay - p.11)
neigh -	See *nay*	(3. ay - p.11)
reign -	See *rain*	(2. ai - p. 9)
rein -	See *rain*	(2. ai - p. 9)
sheik[2] -	See *shake*	(1.a-e - p. 6)
sleigh -	See *slay*	(3. ay - p.11)
their -	See *there*	(7. e-e - p.13)
veil -	See *vale*	(1. a-e - p. 6)
vein -	See *vane*	(1. a-e - p. 7)
weigh -	See *way*	(3. ay - p.11)
weighed* -	past tense form of *to weigh* - *The box weighed a ton.*	

Also: *wade* - *I like to wade in the pond.*

weight -	See *wait*	(2. ai - p.10)

* A root with an inflection

5. ea (great, pear)

bear -	See bare	(1.a-e - p.2)
break -	See brake	(1.a-e - p.1)
great -	See grate	(1.a-e - p.3)
pear -	See pare	(1.a-e - p.4)
steak -	See stake	(1.a-e - p.6)
tear -	See tare	(1.a.e - p.6)
wear -	See ware	(1.a-e - p.7)

6. ey (they, prey)

bey -	See *bay*	(3. ay - p.10)
fey -	See *fay*	(3. ay - p.10)
grey -	See *gray*	(3. ay - p.10)

hey -	See *hay*	(3. ay - p.10)
ley -	See *lay*	(3. ay - p.11)
prey -	See *pray*	(3. ay - p.11)
they're -	See *there*	(7. e-e - p.13)
trey -	See *tray*	(3. ay - p.11)
whey -	See *way*	(3. ay - p.11)

7. e-e (there, where)

ere - See *air*   (2.ai - p.8)
suede - *Dad bought a pair of suede* (leather with a soft nap) *shoes.*
    Also: *swayed* - past tense form of *to sway* - *The building swayed back and forth before it fell.*
there - *Did he put the box over there?* or *There goes Tom with my hat.*
    Also: *their* - *Jim and Mary lost their money.*
    Also: *they're* (contraction of *they are*) *They're not here or anywhere else in the house.*
where - See ware   (1.a-e - p.7)

8. ae   (tael, Gael)

Gael -	See *gale*	(1.a-e - p.3)
tael -	See *tale*	(1.a-e - p.6)

9. au   (gauge)

gauge - See *gage*   (1.a-e - p.3)

10. a   (bass)

bass - See *base*   (1.a-e - p.2)

11. ee   (nee)

nee[1] - See *nay*   (3.ay - p.11)

II - The Short Vowel Sound Of A

Alphabetic Representation	Sound-symbol Representation	Number of Homonyms
1. a	add, flag, tap	72
2. au	laugh	2
3. ai	plaid	0

Total - 74 Homonyms

1. a   add, tap, flag

ant - *I like to watch an ant carry heavy loads.*
   Also: **aunt** - *My aunt came to live with us.* (This word can also be pronounced with the sound heard in *haunt* and *jaunt*.).
band - *The boy played the flute in the band.* or *She put a rubber band around the papers.* or *The people will band together now against the common enemy.*
   Also: **banned** - past tense form of *to ban* - *Why were we banned from watching the show?*
banned * - See **band**   (1.a - p.14)
bach - (Slang) *The young man decided to bach (to live alone)it until the right woman came along.*
   (Alternate form **batch**)
   Also: **batch** - *The truck dropped off a batch of cement.*
batch - See **bach**   (1.a - p.14)
bans* - plural form of *ban* - *Official bans on public gatherings were hated by the people.* or a present tense form of *to ban* - *The government bans the publication of my book.*
   Also: **banns** - only used in plural form - *The banns (an announcement of intended marriage)were announced at the Sunday service.*
banns*   See **bans***   (1.a - p.14)

can't ** - See *cant*   (1.a - p.15)
cant - *None of us understood the speaker's **cant** (hypocritically pious speech)as he talked to us.* or *The hill had a steep **cant**.* or *He is going to **cant** (moralize) when he speaks again.*
  Also: *can't* - a contraction of *can* and *not* - *You **can't** have any more money.*
cache - *The miser hid his **cache** in a hole.* or *Tom will **cache** the gold coins in the basement.*
  Also: *cash* - *Jack had some **cash** in his pocket.* or *Can I **cash** a check here?*
cash - See *cache*   (1.a - p.15)
cast - *The fisherman made an excellent **cast** with his new reel.* or *The molten metal was poured into a **cast**.* or *Dad will **cast** with his new rod.* or *The sailor told me to **cast** off.*
  Also: *caste* - *A **caste** is a hereditary class in Hindu society.* or *The rich man felt obligated to live equally as well as others of his **caste**.* or *In our society, there are a number of **caste** distinctions, including hereditary rank, profession, wealth, etc.*
caste -   See *cast*   (1.a - p.15)
clack - *The wood made a **clack** (noise).* or *The women made an awful **clack** with their gossip.* or *When the wood hits the box it will **clack**.* or *The hens like to **clack** in the yard.*
  Also: *claque* - *The actor hired his own **claque** to applaud at his performances.*
claque - See *clack*   (1.a - p.15)
dam - *The engineers were building a new **dam**.* or *A **dam** is the female parent of a quadruped.* or *Did the beavers **dam** up the stream again?*
  Also: *damn* - *The word **damn** is sometimes used as a curse.* or (Informal) *I just don't give a **damn** any more.* or *The minister likes to **damn** gambling and drinking as sinful actions.*
damn -   See *dam*   (1.a - p.15)
draft - *My room faces north and a **draft** comes through the windows.* or *The **draft** on the furnace is stuck again.* or *The military **draft** took all of the young*

15

men. or *The government will have to draft many men for the war.*
   Also: **draught** - an alternate, Chiefly British variant spelling of **draft**.

franc - *The franc is the basic monetary unit of a large number of countries, including France, Belgium, Chad, Mali, etc.*
   Also: **frank** - *A frank is an official mark placed on a piece of mail so it can be delivered free of charge.* or *The clerk will frank all of the letters.* or *John gave me his frank opinion of my book.*
   Also: **Frank** - a masculine given name, or a nickname for Francis. or *Frank is the name applied to a group of Germanic tribes who lived in the Rhine region during the early Christian era.*

frank - See **franc**   (1.a - p.16)

gaff - *The fisherman used a gaff to help him land the large fish.* or *He had to gaff the shark to get it into the boat.*
   Also: **gaffe** - *The old man committed a terrible gaffe* (a clumsy social error) *and everyone stared.*

gaffe - See **gaff**   (1.a - p.16)

gnat - *A gnat is a tiny winged insect that often bites.*
   Also: **Nat** - an abbreviated form of the proper name Nathan or Nathaniel.

graft - *The man need a skin graft to repair his injury.* or *The dishonest judge took graft* (bribes) *from the unscrupulous police officer.* or *The doctors are going to graft new skin onto my leg.*
   Also: **graphed** - past tense form of *to graph* - *Bill graphed the information onto the chart carefully.*

graphed* - See **graft**   (1.a - p.16)

jam - *The machine had a serious jam.* or *We were late because of the traffic jam.* or (Informal) *The boy is in a jam with the police.* or *Do you like jam on your toast?* or *We had to jam the wedge into the machine to stop it.* or *Why did you jam on the brakes?* or *Mom had to jam the bag to fit everything into it.* or *The musicians like to jam on the spur of the moment.*

Also: *jamb* - *The door jamb can mean the vertical posts of a door or a window.*
jamb -   See *jam*   (1.a - p.16)
knap -   (Regional) *The crest of a hill is sometimes called the knap.* or (British Regional) *I saw them try to knap* (strike sharply at) *it.*
  Also: *nap* - *The baby took a short nap.* or *She brushed the nap off the pile of textiles.* or *Did the old man nap yet?* or *He is working to nap the fabric.*
  Also: *nappe* - *A nappe is a solid sheet of water coming over a dam.* or *The word nappe is one used in both geology and geometry.*
lacks* -   See *lax*   (1.a - p.17)
lam -   (Slang) *The convicts were on the lam.* or (Slang) *The convicts had to lam out of town.* or (Slang) *Dad said he was going to lam* (thrash) *Jim if he didn't behave.*
  Also: *lamb* - *The baby lamb ran around in the pasture with the other lambs.*
lamb -   See *lam*   (1.a - p.17)
lap -   *The baby sat on Mom's lap.* or *The baker will lap the crust over the fruit.* or *The cat went over to lap up the spilled milk.*
  Also: *Lapp* - *A Lapp is an inhabitant of Lapland; it is also the name applied to the Lapp language.*
Lapp -   See *lap*   (1.a - p.17)
laps* -   See *lapse*   (1.a - p.17)
lapse - *His behavior showed a lapse of judgement.* or *After a lapse, the activity began anew.* or *The old woman allowed her insurance policy to lapse.* or *Why did his enthusiasm lapse?*
  Also: *laps* - plural form of *lap* - *They sat on their mothers' laps.* or past tense form of *to lap* - *The kitten laps up the milk from the dish.*
lax -   *Tom was lax about paying his bill.*
  Also: *lacks* - a present tense form of *to lack* - *The child lacks a good home.*
massed* - See *mast*   (1.a - p.17)
mast -   *The ship had a tall mast.*

Also: ***massed*** - past tense form of *to mass* - *The troops were **massed** for an attack.*
mat - *I cleaned my shoes on the **mat** by the door.* or *Mary put her dish on a decorated **mat**.* or *The gymnast landed on a **mat**.* or *The child's hair was stuck in a sticky **mat**.* or *Soon the vines will **mat** the trees and they will be hard to see.*
    Also: ***matte*** - *The word **matte** is used in metallurgy.* or *The girl is going to **matte** the picture.* (Also **mat**)
matte - See ***mat***   (1.a - p.18)
nap - See ***knap***   (1.a - p.17)
nappe - See ***knap***   (1.a - p.17)
Nat - See ***gnat***   (1.a - p.16)
packed* - See ***pact***   (1.a - p.18)
pact - *Six countries signed the new **pact** (agreement).*
    Also: ***packed*** - past tense form of *to pack* - *They left after they **packed** their bags.*
pan - *Mom put all the dishes in the **pan**.* or *All the rainwater drained into a natural desert **pan**.* or *In a flintlock, the **pan** is a small cavity used to hold the powder.* or *The men went to **pan** for gold.* or (Informal) *The critic likes to **pan** (harshly criticize) new plays.* or *Things didn't **pan** out too well this time.*
    Also: ***panne*** - ***Panne*** *is a special finish for satin or velvet that produces a high luster.*
panne - See ***pan***   (1.a - p.18)
passed* - See ***past***   (1.a - p.18)
past - *The time of youth is **past**.* or *When did we go **past** the old barn?* or *He was a man with an honorable **past**.*
    Also: ***passed*** - past tense form of *to pass* - *The two ships **passed** while at sea.*
rack - *I put the silverware on the **rack**.* or *Will you **rack** these cups for me?*
    Also: ***wrack*** - *The storm brought **wrack** and ruin to many.*
rap - *The man gave the door a sharp **rap**.* or *Why did you **rap** on the window?*

Also: **wrap** - *The gift came in a colorful **wrap**.* or *When will you **wrap** the package?*
rapped* - See **rapt** (1.a - p.19)
rapt - *They watched the show with **rapt** attention.*
    Also: **rapped** - past tense form of *to rap* - *The man **rapped** on the door with his fist.*
    Also: **wrapped** - past tense form of *to wrap* - *The cook **wrapped** the meat in tinfoil.*
sac - *A **sac** is a pouchlike structure in a plant or animal.*
    Also: **sack** - *Mom put all the presents in a large **sack**.* or (Slang) *The boss gave him the **sack** (dismissal).* or (Slang) *Bill fell onto his **sack** (bed) and slept.* or *The barbarians will **sack** (plunder) the city.* or *A **sack** is a kind of light, dry, strong wine from Spain.*
sack - See **sac** (1.a - p.19)
scat - (Informal) *We told the animals to **scat**.*
    Also: **skat** - ***Skat** is a card game played by three people.*
skat - See **scat** (1.a - p.19)
staff - *The director was in charge of a large **staff**.* or *The climber carried a sturdy **staff**.* or *The new director will **staff** his company with able people.*
    Also: **staph** - (an abbreviated form of *staphylococcus* (a form of parasitic bacteria) *When did the doctor tell you that you had a **staph** infection?*
staph - See **staff** (1.a - p.19)
tacked* - See **tact** (1.a - p.19)
tacks* - See **tax** (1.a - p.19)
tact - *She did her work with kindness and **tact**.*
    Also: **tacked** - past tense form of *to tack* - *The picture was **tacked** to the wall with two tacks.*
tracked* - See **tract** (1.a - p.19)
tract - *You will find the **tract** in the church entryway.*
    Also: **tracked** - past tense form of *to track* - *The dogs **tracked** down the escaped convict.*
tax - *We had to pay a large **tax** to the city.* or *The mayor will **tax** the people heavily.*
    Also: **tacks** - the plural form of *tack* - *Mom hammered three **tacks** into the wall.*

waffed* - See **waft** ²   (1.a - p.20)
waft ² - *I felt a **waft** of fresh air.* or *The scent of roses will **waft** through the night air.*
    Also: **waffed** - Scottish and British Regional - past tense of *to waff* - *The flag **waffed** in the breeze.*
wax - *The man rubbed the **wax** all over the car.* or *Do you **wax** the table often?*
    Also: **whacks** - past tense form of *to whack* - *The man **whacks** at the box with an old club.*
whacks* - See **wax**   (1.a - p.20)
wrack -   See **rack**   (1.a - p.18)
wrap -   See **rap**   (1.a - p.18)
wrapped* - See **rapt**   (1.a - p.19)
wrath - *The people feared the king's **wrath**.*
    Also: **rathe** - (this word is classed as Archaic now, but when it was in use, it meant *ripening early in the year.* Its most common pronunciation rhymed with *bathe,* but its second most common pronunciation was the same as *wrath.*)
*   A root with an inflection
** A contraction

2. au (laugh)

aunt -   See **ant**   (1.a - p.14)
draught - See **draft**   (1.a - p.15)

3. ai (plaid)

Note: There are no homonyms able to be found for this very rare sound-symbol category.

III - The Long Vowel Sound of E

Alphabetic Representation	Sound-symbol Representation	Number of Homonyms
1. ee	eel, see, feet	58
2. ea	ear, eat, tea	58
3. e-e	cede, gene	14
4. ie	field, piece	12
5. ei	Neil, seize	4
6. e	be, me, we	3
7. i-e	pique	2
8. i	chic	2

Total - 153 Homonyms

1. ee (eel, see, feet)

bee - The child was bitten by a large bee. or Were all the women at the knitting bee?
    Also: be - to be is the infinitive form of the most essential verb in English. Its parts are referred to as *verbs of being,* or sometimes, *copulative verbs.* The 8 parts of this verb are - be-am-is-are-was-were-being-been - *I will be home late tonight*
    Also: Bea - an abbreviated form of the proper name Beatrice.

beech - The beech tree stood in front of the house.
    Also: beach - The children played in the sand at the beach. or The sailor had to beach the old boat.

been [1] - irregular past participle form of the verb to be - Where have you been [2] all week? (The most common pronunciation of this word been [1] is rhymes with *bin.*)
(See bin [VI - 2.i] p.47) See also be (5. e - p.33)
    Also: bean - *I saw a bean on the ground and picked it up. It was a lima bean.* or (Slang) *The*

pitcher tried to bean (intentionally hit)*him with the baseball.*
beer - *The man drank beer with his meal.*
  Also: **bier** - *The coffin was placed on the bier for the family to view.*
beet - *A beet is a dark, red vegetable.*
  Also: **beat** - *The drummer didn't miss beat.* <u>or</u> *Did Mom beat the rug yet?*
breech - *The breech on the gun was broken.* <u>or</u> *He fell and landed on his breech* (buttocks).
  Also: **breach** - *His crime was a serious breach of the law.* <u>or</u> *There was a large breach in the wall of the fort.* <u>or</u> *The troops could not breach the wall.*
cheep - *The young bird made a sound like a cheep.* <u>or</u> *Why does he cheep in his cage?*
  Also: **cheap** - *All the goods on sale were cheap.* <u>or</u> *Bill is a very cheap* (miserly) *person.*
cleek *A cleek is a special kind of golf club.*
  Also: **clique** [1] - *The girls belonged to a clique* (an exclusive group). <u>or</u> *The new people all wanted to clique when they arrived at school.* (**clique** [2] is a homonym of **click**)
creek - *How did the cow get into the creek?* <u>or</u> *Poor Jack is really up the creek* (in an unfortunate position) *now.*
  Also: **creak** - *Did you hear a creak just then?* <u>or</u> *The door is going to creak until I oil it.*
deer - *A large deer came out of the forest.*
  Also: **dear** - *I missed you my dear.* <u>or</u> *Oh dear!* <u>or</u> *Mary is a dear girl.* <u>or</u> *The food at that store was very dear.*
feed - *The cost of feed for the animals is high* <u>or</u> *Will you feed the baby for me?*
  Also: past tense form of *to fee* - *Have you feed the man for your services yet?*
feed* - See **feed**   (1.ee -p.22)
feet - Irregular plural form of the noun *foot* - *Human beings all have two feet.* <u>or</u> *The room was ten feet long and three feet wide.*

Also: **feat** - *The performer demonstrated a **feat** of great grace and daring.*
fees* - See **feeze**   (1.ee - p.23)
feeze - (Regional) *The accident had a terrible **feeze** (impact).* or *The knock on the door caused the thief to **feeze** (flee).*
   Also: **fees** - plural form of **fee** - *The lawyer's **fees** were high.* or a present tense form of **to fee** - *He **fees** his clients each month.*
flee - *The enemy forced us to **flee** from our homes.*
   Also: **flea** - *Is that a **flea** I see on your cat's fur?*
frees* - See **freeze**   (1.ee - p.23)
freeze - *The crops died during the last **freeze**.* or *When will the lake **freeze** this year?*
   Also: **frieze** - *The artist painted a beautiful **frieze** for the new building.*
   Also: **frees** - present tense form of **to free** - *The boy **frees** the animal from the trap.*
Greece - ***Greece** is a republic in southeastern Europe on the southern Balkan Peninsula. It's ancient Greek name was Hellas; its modern Greek name is Ellas.*
   Also: **grease** - ***Grease** is an animal fat or a thick oil lubricant.* or *I am going to **grease** the car now.*
heel - *I hurt my **heel** when I stepped off the step.* or *My shoe needs a new **heel**.* or (Slang) *Why are you even talking to such a disreputable **heel**?* or *The trainer taught the dog to **heel**.* or *Why did the ship **heel** over?*
   Also: **heal** - *Given enough time, his cuts will **heal**.*
keel - *The ship's **keel** was damaged on the rocks.* or *The ship might **keel** over in this wind.*
   Also: **Kiel** - *The name of a large city in Germany.*
knee - *I hurt my **knee** when I knelt down.*
   Also: **nee**[2] - rhymes with the word **knee**. *It is used to identify the maiden name of a married woman, as in Mrs. Mary Jones, **nee**[2] Smith.* (Its most common pronunciation rhymes with **nay**.)
kneed* - See **need**   (1.ee - p.24)
kneel - *Why do people **kneel** at the altar?*
   Also: ***Neil** is the name of my best friend.*

Also: **Neal** - a variant spelling for **Neil**.

lee - The **lee** side of a ship is the side sheltered from the wind. or We sat on the **lee** side.
Also: **lea** - (Poetic) - A **lea** is a meadow or grassland. (A variant spelling of this word is **ley** and is pronounced to rhyme with **lay**.)

leech - A **leech** is a kind of blood-sucking worm. or The sail needed a new **leech**.
Also: **leach** - Can you please get me some new **leach** for my filter? or If we allow the water to **leach** through the soil, it will be cleansed.

leek - The **leek** is a plant that produces a vegetable that tastes much like an onion.
Also: **leak** - Does that faucet have a **leak**? or Did the water **leak** all over the floor.

leer - The young woman didn't like the **leer** that you had on your face just then. or If you **leer** at her, she might slap your face.
Also: **Lear** - the protagonist in Shakespeare's *King Lear*.

meet - Why was the track **meet** held in the old school. or When did you **meet** Jim? or Did the new house **meet** with your expectations?
Also: **meat** - They cooked the **meat** of the animal over an open fire.
Also: Why did the judge **mete** out such a harsh punishment?

nee[2] - See **knee** (1.ee - p.23)

need - The poor children were in great **need**. or That child has a great **need** for love and affection. or Are we going to **need** candles for dinner tonight?
Also: **knead** - The baker had to **knead** the flour into a moist dough.
Also: **kneed** (Slang) past tense form of *to knee* - The football player **kneed** the runner as he passed him.

pee - Although its use is classified as Vulgar, it is a very commonly used word, especially by, and with, children, and means *to urinate,* or , urine itself.
Also: **pea** - A **pea** is green and grows on a vine in a pod. or May I have another bowl of **pea** soup?

peek - *The small child moved his hands and took a quick* ***peek*** *at the gift.* or *She told them not to* ***peek*** *at the animals.*
   Also: **peak** - *The man climbed to the very* ***peak*** *of the mountain.* or *The runner didn't want to* ***peak*** *too soon.*
   Also: **pique** - *His* ***pique*** (resentment from wounded pride) *over the affair was obvious.* or *I will* ***pique*** *him with this insult.* or *The food aroma will* ***pique*** (arouse) *his appetite.*
peel - *I ate the* ***peel*** *of the apple.* or *The baker moved the loaves in the oven with a* ***peel****.* or *Will you* ***peel*** *this potato for me?*
   Also: **peal** - *I could hear the loud* ***peal*** *of the bells in the tower.* or *The minister will* ***peal*** *the bells after the service.*
peer - *A* ***peer*** *is one who is equal in class or ranking.* or *A duke or an earl is referred to as a* ***peer*** *and is considered a nobleman in Britain.* or *Why is the little boy trying to* ***peer*** *through the little window?*
   Also: **pier** - *We walked down the* ***pier*** *and boarded the boat.* or *He looked at the weakened* ***pier*** *which was supposed to hold up the bridge.*
queen - *The* ***queen*** *sat on the throne next to the king.* or *This bee is a* ***queen*** *in this hive.* or (Slang) *An effeminate male homosexual is referred to as a* ***queen****.* or *I am going to* ***queen*** *this chess piece.*
   Also: **quean** - (Scottish) *A* ***quean*** *is a young woman.*
reed - *Mother put a tall* ***reed*** *into the vase.* or *The* ***reed*** *in my clarinet is broken.*
   Also: **read** - *Did you* ***read*** *my new book yet?*
   Also: **rede** - (Archaic) *A name for good advice, or, the act of giving advice or counsel.*
reek - *The rotting fish had a strong* ***reek*** *to it.* or *Spoiled food will* ***reek*** *if left in the sun.*
   Also: **wreak** - *The king is going to* ***wreak*** *his vengeance upon the people.*
reel - *Tom got a new* ***reel*** *for his fishing pole.* or *Can you* ***reel*** *in that fish all alone?*

Also: Although the preferred pronunciation for this word is in two syllables - **re al** (ree ul), it may also be pronounced to rhyme with **reel** - *Annie has a real talent for singing.*
Also: **riel** - *The riel is the basic monetary unit of Cambodia.* (Properly **ri el** [ree ul]. See **real**)

see - *A bishop rules over a jurisdiction which is referred to as a see.* <u>or</u> *Can you see Peggy from the window?* <u>or</u> *I can't quite see him as president of our class.*
Also: **sea** - *Dad went to sea aboard a gray cruiser.* <u>or</u> *The word sea refers to a body water which contains salt.*

sees* - See *seize* (5.ei - p.32)

seed - *When will we plant the grass seed this year.* <u>or</u> *He carried the seed of his ancestry into battle.* <u>or</u> *The farmer went into his fields to seed them for the coming growing season.*
Also: **cede** - *The government decided to cede* (yield or grant) *the territory rather than go to war.*

seek - *The young man went to seek his fortune in the big city.*
Also: **Sikh** - *A Sikh is an adherent of Sikhism, a monotheistic Hindu religious sect.*

seem - *Does it seem like a long time since we got here?* <u>or</u> *You seem to be honest, but you're not.*
Also: **seam** - *Each seam fitted the other perfectly.* <u>or</u> *She can seam them together on her sewing machine.*

seen - irregular past participle of *to see* - *Billy has not been seen for two weeks.*
Also: **scene** - *The director placed the actors for the next scene.* <u>or</u> (Slang) *The scene is where all the exciting action takes place.*

sheer - *The truck had to sheer to the left to avoid the car.* <u>or</u> *The fabric was so sheer, we could see through it.* <u>or</u> *It was sheer luck that we won the game.*
Also: **shear** - *How did he shear the wool from that sheep so quickly?* <u>or</u> *The force of the pressure could shear the nut from its bolt.*

sleeve - One *sleeve* in the jacket was longer than the other. or The tailor worked to *sleeve* the coat.
  Also: *sleave* - All of the thread was in a *sleave* (tangle). or I worked hard to *sleave* (separate) all the tangled threads.
steel - The tall building was made entirely of *steel* and glass. or The soldier had a will of *steel*.
  Also: *steal* - The price of the dress was so low she thought it was a *steal*. or The man went to jail because he tried to *steal* my car.
steer - Why did the rancher raise only one *steer*? or The captain helped me to *steer* the ship during the storm.
  Also: *stere* - A *stere* is a unit of volume equal to one cubic meter.
steeve - A *steeve* is a derrick used on a ship to store cargo. or We had to *steeve* the cargo in the ship's hold.
  Also: *Steve* - an abbreviated form of the name Steven or Stephen.
sweet - The children love to eat *sweet* food. or She is a very *sweet* woman.
  Also: *suite* - The queen had an entire *suite* of attendants. or The hotel gave us a full *suite* of rooms for our vacation. or The orchestra played a piano *suite* last evening.
tee - The golfer hit the golf ball off the *tee*. or Will you please *tee* my ball for me because I have a bad back. or (Slang) When will your election campaign *tee* off? or You really *tee* me off. (to make one angry)
  Also: *tea* - Can you grow *tea* on that hillside? or There are many different kinds of *tea*. or In many places, principally in Great Britain, *tea* is an afternoon refreshment of cakes and tea.
teem - A drop of water seems to *teem* with life. or It looks like it is going to *teem* (rain very hard) soon.
  Also: *team* - Our *team* had a great season and we won all of our games. or I think I will *team* up with my friends.

wee - *The wee* (small) *child went ahead of the class.* or *They came home in the wee* (early)*hours of the morning.*
Also: *we went to school to meet Tom.*
week - *There are seven days in one week.*
Also: *weak* - *The old man was so weak with hunger that he couldn't walk.*
ween - (Archaic) *I ween (suppose) anything is possible.*
Also: *wean* - *The young mother tried to wean her baby away from the bottle.*
wheel - *The wheel of the wagon was stuck in the mud.* or *He could not wheel his bike home.* (Although the digraph *wh* is properly pronounced as *hw*, as in *wheel* [*hweel*], many people, from diverse educational backgrounds, pronounce it as though it began with the simple individual sound for *w*.)
Also: *weal* - *The teacher worked long and hard for the common weal* (welfare).
Also: *wheal* - *A wheal is a small acute swelling on the skin.* (See *wheel*)
wheeled* - See *wield* (4.ie - p.32)
* A root with an inflection

2. ea   ear, eat, tea

Bea -   See *bee*   (1. ee - p.21)
beach -   See *beech*   (1. ee - p.21)
bean -   See *been*   (1. ee - p.21)
beat -   See *beet*   (1. ee - p.22)
breach - See *breech* (1. ee - p.22)
cheap - See *cheepq* (1. ee - p.22)
creak -   See *creek*   (1. ee - p.22)
deal - *The salesman gave me a good deal and I bought the car.* or *If you don't pay attention in some card games, you will miss your deal.* or *Is it my turn to deal the cards?*

Also: *dele* - *A dele is a typesetter's sign to remove certain material.* or *The typesetter had to dele some material from the type.*
dear -   See *deer*   (1. ee - p.22)
eave - always used in its plural form as *eaves,* an *eave* is the projecting overhang at the lower edge of a roof.
Also: *An eve is the period immediately preceding a certain event: the eve of war, or Christmas Eve.*
feat -   See *feet*   (1. ee - p.22)
flea -   See *flee*   (1. ee - p.23)
grease - See *Greece*   (1. ee - p.23)
heal -   See *heel*   (1. ee - p.23)
hear - *The man was deaf and could not hear the bells.*
Also: *here - I will sit here and you can sit there.*
jean -   See *gene*   (3. e-e - p.31)
knead - See *need*   (1. ee - p.24)
leaf - *The tree held on to its last leaf.* or *I like to leaf through new books.*
Also: *lief - He would lief* (willingly)*go now as later.*
lea -   See *lee*   (1.ee - p.24)
leach - See *leech*   (1.ee - p.24)
leak -   See *leek*   (1.ee - p.24)
lean - *The boxer was strong and lean.* or *I like beef that is very lean.* or*Don't lean over the cliff or you'll fall off.*
Also: *lien - The lawyer had a lien placed on the property so it couldn't be sold.*
Lear -   See *leer*   (1.ee - p.24)
leased* - See *least*   (2.ea - p.29)
least - *He is the least likely person I can imagine for this job.* or *I have the least money of any of the boys.*
Also: *leased* - past tense form of *to lease* - *The land was leased for a small amount of money.*
mead - *They drink mead* (a beverage made from fermented honey and water) *from a large mug.*
Also: *Mede - A Mede was an inhabitant of ancient Media.*

mean - *The mean old man took the child's toys away from him.* <u>or</u> *What did he mean when he said those words?*
    Also: *mien* - *The count was a person of noble mien* (bearing or carriage).

meat -	See *meet*	(1.ee - p.24)
pea -	See *pee*	(1.ee - p.24)
peace -	See *piece*	(4.ie - p.32)
peak -	See *peek*	(1.ee - p.25)
peal -	See *peel*	(1.ee - p.25)

peat - *The old woman heated her home with peat from the bog.*
    Also: *Pete* - an abbreviated form of the name Peter.
pleas* - See *please*   (2.ea - p.30)
please - *He didn't say please when he asked for more food.* <u>or</u> *The boy always tried to please his dad.*
    Also: plural form of *plea* - *No one would listen to his pleas for mercy.*

quean -	See *queen*	(1.ee - p.25)
read -	See *reed*	(1.ee - p.25)
real -	See *reel*	(1.ee - p.25)
sea -	See *see*	(1.ee - p.26)

seal - *The seal in the circus did many tricks.* <u>or</u> *The king placed the royal seal on the letter.* <u>or</u> *They went out in their boat to seal* (to hunt for seals). <u>or</u> *When did you seal the envelope?*
    Also: *ceil* - *My work is to ceil.* (to make a ceiling for, or to provide the inner planking for a ship).

seam -	See *seem*	(1.ee - p.26)

sear - *His elbow had a sear on it.* <u>or</u> *The cowboy was going to sear the hide with a hot iron..*
    Also: *sere* - A variant spelling of *sear*, especially as - *The sere* (dry) *desert air stifled him.*

seas* -	See *seize*	(5.ei - p.32)
seat -	See *cete*	(3.e-e - p.31)
shear -	See *sheer*	(1.ee - p.26)
sleave -	See *sleeve*	(1.ee - p.27)
steal -	See *steel*	(1.ee - p.27)
tea -	See *tee*	(1.ee - p.27)
team -	See *teem*	(1.ee - p.27)

tear - *A salty tear fell from her eye.* or *When you have a cold, your eyes tend to tear.*
    Also: *tier* - *We sat in the third tier in the balcony of the theater.* or *The photographer had to tier the class for the photo.*
teas* - See *tease*   (2.ea - p.31)
tease - *Jimmy is a terrible tease.* or *Why do they tease you so much?*
    Also: plural form of *tea* - *There are many teas on the shelf to choose from.*
weak - See *week*   (1.ee - p.28)
weal - See *wheel*   (1.ee - p.28)
weald - See *wield*   (4.ie - p.32)
wean - See *ween*   (1.ee - p.28)
weave - *That coat has a very fine weave.* or *The tailor will weave a robe for the queen.*
    Also: *we've***- a contraction of *we* and *have* *We've been there already and we like it.*
wheal - See *wheel*   (1.ee - p.28)
wreak - See *reek*   (1.ee - p.25)
* A root with an inflection
** A contraction

3. e-e   (cede, gene)

cede - See *seed*   (1.ee - p.26)
cete - *A cete is a company of badgers.*
    Also: *Tom fell off the broken seat.* or *The ice skater fell on his seat* (buttocks). or *The capital city is the seat of authority.* or *How did that man get a seat on the stock exchange?* or *The usher will seat the guests.*
dele - See *deal*   (2.ea - p.28)
eve - See *eave*   (2.ea - p.29)
gene - *A gene is a functional hereditary unit located on a chromosome.*
    Also: *jean* - *Jean is a kind of strong, heavy twilled cotton used in making work clothes and uniforms.*
    Also: *Jean* - a feminine given name.

here -	See *hear*	(2.ea - p.29)
Mede -	See *mead*	(2.ea - p.29)
mete -	See *meet*	(1.ee - p.24)
Pete -	See *peat*	(2.ea - p.30)
scene -	See *seen*	(1.ee - p.26)
sere -	See *sear*	(2.ea - p.30)
stere -	See *steer*	(1.ee - p.27)
Steve -	See *steeve*	(1.ee - p.27)

4. ie   field, piece

bier -	See *beer*	(1.ee - p.22)
frieze -	See *freeze*	(1.ee - p.23)
Kiel -	See *keel*	(1.ee - p.23)
lief -	See *leaf*	(2.ea - p.29)
lien -	See *lean*	(2.ea - p.29)
mien -	See *mean*	(2.ea - p.30)

piece - *May I have a small piece of pie?* or *If we try, we can piece the puzzle together.*
    Also: *peace* - *The two sides tried to make peace.*

pier -	See *peer*	(1.ee - p.25)
riel -	See *reel*	(1.ee - p.25)
tier -	See *tear*	(2.ea - p.31)

wield - *The ruler will wield his power to end the revolt.*
    Also: *weald* - (Chiefly British) *The cattle roamed over the weald* (open rolling upland).
    Also: past tense form of *to wheel* - *The small boy wheeled his tricycle down the road.*

5. ei   Neil, seize

ceil -	See *seal*	(2.ea - p.30)
Neil -	See *kneel*	(1.ee - p.23)
seise -	See *seize*	(5.ei - p.32)

seize - *The government is going to seize all of my property.* or *It was either great pressure or high temperature that caused the engine to seize.*

Also: *seise* - (Law) A variant spelling can be used when the meaning of *seize* pertains to a legal seizure or confiscation.
Also: *sees* - past tense form of *to see* - *The girl sees her dog in the road.*
Also: *seas* - plural noun form of *sea* - *There are many seas all over the world.*
sheik[1] - *A sheik is a Moslem religious leader or the leader of an Arab family or clan.*
(*sheik*[2] is pronounced as though it rhymed with **shake**. See **shake** I [a-e] - p.12)
Also: *chic* - *She demonstrated a great deal of chic (stylishness).* or *The model wore a very chic (sophisticated) outfit to the party.*
weir - *The old weir across the stream has been in use for years to catch and hold fish.* or *Is the weir still used to raise the water level for the race?*
Also: *we're* **-a contraction of *we* and *are* - *We're going home as soon as possible.*
** A contraction

6. e (be, we)

be -	See *bee*	(1.ee - p.21)
we -	See *wee*	(1.ee - p.28)
we're** -	See *weir*	(5.ei - p.33)
we've** -	See *weave*	(2.ea - p.31)

** A contraction

7. i-e (pique)

clique -	See *cleek*	(1.ee - p.22)
pique -	See *peek*	(1.ee - p.25)

8. i (chic)

chic -	See *sheik*[1]	(5.ei - p.33)
Sikh -	See *seek*	(1.ee - p.26)

IV - The Short Vowel Sound of E

Alphabetic Representation	Sound-symbol Representation	Number of Homonyms
1. e	edge, leg, ten	37
2. ea	bread, tread	2

Total - 39 Homonyms

1. e   edge, leg, ten

bell - *I heard the bell ring three times.* or *Did the diver go deep into the ocean in his diving bell?* or *The vet had to bell the skittish cat for me.*
    Also: *belle* - *Miranda is a real southern belle* (an attractive and admired girl or woman). or *She was the belle of the ball.*
belle -   See *bell*   (1.e - p.34)
bred - irregular past tense form of *to breed* - *The race horse was bred for speed and stamina.*
    Also: *bread* - *White bread is my favorite.* or *The cook said to bread the meat before frying it.*
blessed* - See *blest*   (1.e - p.34)
blest - alternate spelling of the irregular past tense form and past participle of *to bless* - *The man was blest with happy children.*
    Also: past tense form of *to bless* - *The minister blessed the congregation.*
cell - *The prisoner went to his cell.* or *The cell is the smallest biological unit of structure capable of independent functioning.* or *The cell in my battery did not work.*
    Also: *sell* - *He is going to sell his old car.*
cent -   *The child had one cent to spend on candy.*
    Also: *scent* - *The scent of the perfume was very strong.* or *The dog caught the scent of a fox in the air.* or *I scent danger in the air.*
    Also: *sent* - irregular past tense form of *to send* - *We sent them a package through the mail.*

cents* - See *sense* (1.e - p.36)
check - *My boss wrote a large check for me.* or *The wall served as a check against the advancing troops.* or *The player gave me a stiff body check.* or *The new dam helped to check the raging water.* or *Can I check my hat here?*
 Also: *Czech* - *A Czech is a native of Czechoslovakia; it is also the name of their language.*
Czech - See *check* (1.e - p.35)
flecks* - See *flex* (1.e - p.35)
flex - *Why did the man try to flex his muscles?*
 Also: *flecks* - plural form of *fleck* - *I saw flecks of paint on the floor.* or a present tense form of *to fleck* - *The painter tried to fleck the new paint.*
guessed* - See *guest* (1.e - p.35)
guest - *Dad brought home a guest for dinner.* or *The guest speaker was late.*
 Also: *guessed* - past tense form of *to guess* - *They guessed wrong about the time of arrival.*
led - irregular past tense form of *to lead* - *The group were led up the side of the steep hill.*
 Also: *lead* - *Lead is a soft and malleable metallic element.* or *The lead in my pencil broke again.*
let - *Bob let it be known that he was unhappy.* or *Our house had to let sign on the gate.*
 Also: *Lett* - *A person from Latvia is a Lett.*
Lett - See *let* (1.e - p.35)
reck - *The driver does not reck* (take heed of) *danger.*
 Also: *wreck* - *The car was a total wreck.* or *They are going to wreck that beautiful old home today.*
red - *The color red is my favorite.*
 Also: *read* - irregular past tense form of *to read* - *The teacher read a story to her class.*
rest - *Grandmother is going to take a rest now.* or *The rest of the team were late.*
 Also: *wrest* - *A small group of men tried to wrest control of power from the government.*
retch - *The bad taste made me want to retch* (try to vomit).
 Also: *wretch* - *That man is the terrible wretch who beat the small child.*

scend - *The scend* (rising movement) *made the ship move quickly.* or *The ship will scend* (heave upward) *on the wave.* (Variant spelling *send*)
    Also: *send* - *The principle is going to send us home.*
sell -   See *cell*   (1.e - p.34)
send -   See *scend*   (1.e - p.36)
scent -   See *cent*   (1.e - p.34)
scents* - See *sense*   (1.e - p.36)
sense - *His conversation made no sense.* or *What did you sense when you went inside?*
    Also: *cents* - plural form of *cent* - *The price of the candy was ten cents.*
    Also: *scents* - plural form of *scent* - *The woman wears lovely scents.* or a present tense form of *to scent* - *The dog scents an animal in the bush.*
sent -   See *cent*   (1.e - p.34)
sexed* - See *sext*   (1.e - p.36)
sext - *Sext is the fourth of the canonical hours; it is also the period of time set aside for prayer during these hours, usually the sixth hour or noon.*
    Also: *sexed* - past tense form of *to sex* - *The vet sexed* (determined the sex of) *the young chickens.*
wen - *The doctor removed a small wen* (cyst) *from the woman's scalp.*
    Also: *when* - *When will the train arrive?*
wet - *The firemen had to wet down the burning embers.* or *My shoes were all wet from the rain.*
    Also: *whet* - *The man in the shop is going to whet* (sharpen) *my knife on the stone.*
when -   See *wen*   (1.e - p.36)
whet -   See *wet*   (1.e - p.36)
wreck -   See *reck*   (1.e - p.35)
wrest -   See *rest*   (1.e - p.35)
wretch - See *retch*   (1.e - p.35)
* A root with an inflection

2. ea   bread, tread
bread -   See *bred*   (1.e - p.34)
lead -   See *led*   (1.e - p.35)
read -   See *red*   (1.e - p.35)

V - The Long Vowel Sound of I

Alphabetic Representation	Sound-symbol Representation	Number of Homonyms
1. i-e	ice, fine, hide	42
2. i	I, fight, high	26
3. y-e	rhyme, thyme	7
4. ie	die, lie, tie	7
5. ye	lye, rye	5
6. y	by, fly	6
7. ei	height, sleight	3
8. uy	buy, guy	1
9. oi	choir	1
10. eye	eye	1
11. aye	aye	1

Total - 101 Homonyms

1. i-e   (ice, fine, hide)

bite - *The dentist said I have a good **bite**.* or *We stopped at the restaurant for a quick **bite**.* or *The snake will **bite** if you are not careful.*
   Also: **bight** - *The rope has a large **bight** (loop) in it.* or *A **bight** is a bend or a curve in the shoreline.* or *He is going to **bight** (secure with a loop) the package so it won't fall.*
blite - *A word used in combination with another designator, as in the strawberry **blite** (a weedy plant).*
   Also: **blight** - *A sudden **blight** caused the leaves to wither and die.* or *This bad weather is going to **blight** the entire crop.*
chime - *He used a **chime** to strike the bell.* or *I like the sound of a **chime**.* or *The bell will **chime** when I strike it.* or *Why did they all **chime** in while we were there?*
   Also: **chyme** - ***Chyme** is the thick semi-fluid mass of partly digested food that passes from the stomach to the duodenum.*

cite - See *site*   (1.i-e - p.40)
clime - (Poetic) *The man departed for a more hospitable clime* (climate).
> Also: *climb* - *The climb to the top was difficult.* or *We are going to climb the mountain in the morning.*

dine - *Where shall we dine this evening?*
> Also: *dyne* - *In physics, a dyne is a unit of force.*

fined* - See *find*   (2.i - p.42)

guide - *Our guide on the African Safari got lost.* or *The guide that came with the machine is useless.* or *I will guide you through the deep forest to your home.*
> Also: *guyed* - past tense form of *to guy* - *The tall tree was guyed* (fastened) *with a strong rope.*

guise - *The man showed himself in a false guise.*
> Also: *guys* - (Informal) *All of the guys* (fellows) *came to the party.* or plural form of *guy* - *The pole was held tightly by two guys* (ropes or cables) or a present tense form of *to guy* - *The worker guys the flag pole.*

hide - *An elephant has a tough hide.* or *A hide was an Old English measure.* or *She is going to hide all the silverware in the basement.*
> Also: *hied* - past tense form of *to hie* - *The noblemen hied* (hastened or hurried) *to their own castles for safety.*
> Also: *Hyde* - (Informal) *Jekyll and Hyde is a term used to describe a person whose behavior alternates between pleasantness and unpleasantness.* (It comes from a story by R.L.Stevenson (1886) *The Strange Case of Dr. Jekyll and Mr. Hyde.*)

hire - *Is this taxi for hire at present?* or *The boss didn't want to hire my father.*
> Also: *higher* - the comparative adjective form of *high* - *This hill is high, but that one is higher.*

mined* - See *mind*   (2.i - p.43)

mite - *A mite is a parasite that infests food and carries disease.* or *A mite is a very small amount of money, as in "a widow's mite".*

Also: **might** - *He hit the ball with all his **might**.* or *The entire **might** of the army was thrown at the advancing enemy.* or past tense form of *may* - *I **might** have gone had it been a nice day.*

pride - *He stayed in the race because of the **pride** he felt in himself.* or *A group or company of lions is called a **pride**.* or *I **pride** myself on my beautiful garden.*
  Also: **pried** - past tense form of *to pry* - *How was the safe **pried** open?*

prize - *Who won first **prize**?* or *I will always **prize** your friendship.*
  Also: **pries** - present tense form of *to pry* - *The fireman **pries** open the door.*

quire - *I bought a **quire** (one half ream) of paper.* or *A **quire** is a set of all leaves required for a book.* or *I am going to **quire** the book.*
  Also: **choir** - *The **choir** sang at the church service.* or *We sat in the **choir**.* or *I am going to **choir** with the whole group.*

rime - ***Rime** is frost or an ice coating on grass and trees, and it is also called hoarfrost.* or *The low temperature will **rime** the hillside.*
  Also: **rhyme** - *I enjoy poetry with a **rhyme** to it.* or *We sat together and tried to **rhyme** the lines.*

rite - *The pastor conducted the **rite** of baptism.* or *He is a member of the Anglican **Rite**.*
  Also: *I prefer to **write** with my left hand.* or *Why did he decide to **write** that story?*
  Also: **right** - *Did they have the **right** to vote?* or *We sat on the **right** side of the room.* or *He was **right** and I was wrong.*
  Also: **wright** - *A **wright** is a person who constructs things, such as a play**wright**, or a ship**wright**, or a wheel**wright**.*

side - *He sat on the left **side** of the class.* or *One **side** of the triangle was an inch longer than the other two.* or *Dad will **side** with his children in the dispute.* or *The men came to **side** (to put sides or siding on) the old barn.*

Also: ***sighed*** - past tense form of *to sigh* - *She **sighed** as she left the room.*

sine - *The **sine** is a term used to signify a mathematical function.*

Also: ***sign*** - *A **sign** is a signal used to convey an idea.* or *We looked at the man as he painted the **sign**.* or *She forgot to **sign** her name.*

site - *The **site** of the new building was in an old field.*

Also: ***cite*** - *The writer is going to **cite** your book as a reference.* or *Why did the general **cite** you for bravery?*

Also: ***sight*** - *My **sight** is not as good as it used to be.* or *The man was in my line of **sight**.* or *You are a **sight** for sore eyes.* or *When will we **sight** land?*

size - *What is the **size** of your neck?* or *That's about the **size** of the situation.* or ***Size** is a material used to glaze porous materials.* or *I will cut the material to **size**.* or *He tried to **size** up the situation.*

Also: ***sighs*** - plural form of *sigh* - *We could hear their **sighs** in the next room.* or present tense form of *to sigh* - *The man **sighs** as the judge sentences him.*

spice - *A **spice** is a vegetable substance that is used to flavor food or beverages.* or *Mom wanted to **spice** up the sauce.*

Also: ***speiss*** - ***Speiss** is a basic arsenic or antimony compound.*

sprite - *The story was all about a little **sprite** (an elf or supernatural being); it is also the name given to the green woodpecker.*

Also: ***spright*** - a variant spelling for **sprite**.

stile - *A **stile** is a set of steps used for getting over a wall or a fence.* or *A **stile** is a vertical member of a frame in a door or window sash.*

Also: ***style*** - *Do you like her new hair **style**?* or *Tanya is going to **style** my hair for me in a new way.*

tide - *Is the ocean at high or low tide now?* or *The general's attack turned the whole tide of battle.* or *This small amount of money will not tide us over the bad period.*
  Also: *tied* - past tense form of *to tie* - *The man's hands and feet were tied.*
time - *I will be home on time.* or *What time is it?* or *The teacher will time the class to see who finishes the test first.*
  Also: *thyme* - *I use thyme to make my food taste better.*
tine - *A tine can be a branch of a deer's antlers or a prong of a fork.*
  Also: *Tyne* - *The Tyne is a river in northern England.*
tire - *I need a new tire for my car.* (Also British *tyre*) or *I never tire of hearing Annie sing.*
  Also: *Tyre* - *Tyre was the capital of ancient Phoenicia.*
vice - *The man had a serious vice* (a moral failing). or *He will serve as the vice principal until I am well again.*
  Also: *vise* - *The wood was held tightly in the vise.* or *I will vise the metal while you turn it.* (Variant spelling *vice*)
vise -   See *vice*   (1.i-e - p.41)
while - *Will you stay for a while so we can talk?* or *It's not worth my while to stay here.* or *It is pleasant to while away the hours talking over old times.* or (conjunction) *While it is raining, we will stay inside.*
  Also: *wile* - *Your wile did not succeed in tricking me.* or *The evil man tries to wile* (entice) *the innocent.* or (a different word, but one having the same meaning used above in *to while*) *We can wile away this fine afternoon at the lake.*
whiled* - See *wild*   (2.i - p.43)
whine -   See *wine*   (1.i-e - p.42)
whined* - See *wind*   (2.i - p.44)

white - *The color of snow is white.* or *An egg has two parts, the yolk and the white.* or *The white whale was hunted widely.*
    Also: (Archaic) *A wight was a name once used for a human being or a creature.* or (Obsolete) *The knight was wight* (brave).
wile - See *while*   (1.i-e - p.41)
wiled* - See *wild*   (2.i - p.43)
wine - *Do you like to drink red or white wine with dinner?* or *The coach will wine and dine the team if they win the playoff game.*
    Also: *whine* - *I heard a low whine coming from behind the wall.* or *The boy is going to whine to his father.*
wined* - See *wind*   (2.i - p.44)
wise - *In no wise* (way or manner of doing) *is your opinion correct.* or *How did she become so wise?*
    Also: *whys* - plural form of *why* - *The whys* (underlying cause or intention) *of the judge's opinion were difficult to understand.*
write - See *rite*   (1.i-e - p.39)
* A root with an inflection

2. i   (I, fight, high)

bight - See *bite*   (1.i-e - p.37)
blight - See *blite*   (1.i-e - p.37)
climb - See *clime*   (1.i-e - p.38)
find - *Discovering oil on that land was a great find.* or *Where will we go to find water?*
    Also: *fined* - past tense form of *to fine* - *Why was she fined so heavily for such a minor crime?*
hi - See *hie*   (3.ie - p.44)
high - See *hie*   (3.ie - p.44)
higher* - See *hire*   (1.i-e - p.38)
I - *I* - first person singular personal pronoun form - *I need a new hat.*
    Also: *aye* - *Aye is a word used to give an affirmative vote.* (Also spelled *ay*)

Also: *eye* - *My eye is almost closed from a swelling.* or *He tried to eye what I was doing, but he couldn't see my paper.*
knight - See *night*   (2.i - p.43)
might - See *mite*   (1.i-e - p.38)
mind - *That boy has a mind of his own to think with.* or *Dad stayed home to mind the baby.*
     Also: *mined* - past tense form of *to mine* - *The men mined coal from the old mine.*
night - *The cat stayed out all night.* or *The dark night of imprisonment was over.*
     Also: *knight* - *A knight was a man noble of mind and body.* or *A knight is a chess piece that is represented as a horse's head.* or *The king is going to knight Sir John next week.*
pi -   See *pie*   (4.ie - p.45)
*psi*² -   See *sigh*   (2.i - p.43)
right - See *rite*   (1.i-e - p.39)
rind - *The rind is a name used for the tough outer covering of bark, some fruit, or even cheese or bacon.*
     Also: *rynd* - *A rynd is an iron bar supporting an upper millstone.*
sigh - *The woman breathed a sigh when she saw her child.* or *I think she is going to sigh again.*
     Also: *psi*² (sie) - the 23rd letter of the Greek alphabet. (In *psi*¹ the consonant p is pronounced.)
sighed* - See *side*   (1.i-e - p.39)
sighs* - See *size*   (1.i-e - p.40)
sight -   See *site*   (1.i-e - p.40)
sign -   See *sine*   (1.i-e - p.40)
slight - *Forgetting her birthday was a major slight.* or *They are going to slight him by not inviting him to the party.* or *I have a slight cold.*
     Also: *sleight* - *The magician was well known for his sleight of hand* (tricks).
spright - See *sprite*   (1.i-e - p.40)
wight -   See *white*   (1.i-e - p.42)
wild - *Many animals still live in the wild.* or *Why does he have such a wild look on his face.*

Also: ***wiled*** - past tense form of *to wile* - *They wiled the man with their evil trickery.*
Also: ***whiled*** - *I whiled away the hours happily.*
wind - *Can you give that winch a **wind** for me?* or *I could not **wind** the clock any further.* or *I like to **wind** down at the end of the day.*
Also: ***wined*** - past tense form of *to wine* - *We were **wined** and dined by our host.*
Also: ***whined*** - *When the old dog **whined**, I looked out the window.*
wright - See ***rite***   (1.i-e - p.39)
* A root with an inflection   ** A contraction

3. y-e   (rhyme, thyme)

chyme -	See ***chime***	(1.i-e - p.37)
dyne -	See ***dine***	(1.i-e - p.38)
Hyde -	See ***hide***	(1.i-e - p.38)
rhyme -	See ***rime***	(1.i-e - p.39)
style -	See ***stile***	(1.i-e - p.40)
thyme -	See ***time***	(1.i-e - p.41)
Tyne -	See ***tine***	(1.i-e - p.41)
Tyre -	See ***tire***	(1.i-e - p.41)

4. ie   (die, lie, tie)

die - *A **die** is a device for cutting out, stamping, or forming material, especially metal.* or *He lost one **die** of the pair of dice his father gave him.* or *The metal worker is going to **die** some new coins today.* or *Does the old man know that he is going to **die** (cease living)?*
    Also: ***dye*** - *Where did you get red **dye** for that sweater?* or *Who is going to **dye** this material?*
hie - *We must **hie** (hasten) to the castle and save the king.*
    Also: ***hi*** - (Informal) Interjection - ***Hi**! How are you?* or (British) ***Hi**! Look where you're going!*

Also: *high* - *The plane was flying high in order to get weather data.* or *The ball flew high up into the air.* or *The singer hit a high note.* or *The high priest went into the temple.*
Also: *heigh* - Interjection - *Heigh-ho! I'm worn out.* (Also pronounced to rhyme with *hay*)

hied* - (From *to hie* - See *hide*   1.i-e - p.38)
lie - The *lie* is the position in which a thing is situated, such as the place where a golf ball comes to a stop. or *Why did you tell your mother a lie?* or *I think I will lie down for a rest now.* or *It is deceitful to lie to those who trust you.*
Also: *lye* - *Be careful or the lye will burn your skin.*
pie - *He ate a large piece of the fruit pie that Mary made.* or *A pie is a type of bird, such as a magpie.*
Also: *pi* - *Pi is the 16th letter of the Greek alphabet.* or *Pi is a transcendental number representing 3.14159.* or *Pi is a term used by printers to represent any amount of print that has been thrown together randomly.* (Variant spellings of the verb form for the final meaning are *to pi, or to pie.*)
pried* - See *pride*   (1.i-e - p.39)
pries* - See *prize*   (1.i-e - p.39)
tied* - (From *to tie* - See *tide* 1.i-e - 41)
* A root with an inflection

5. ye   (lye, rye)

bye -   See *by*   (6.y - p.45)
dye -   See *die*   (4.ie - p.44)
lye -   See *lie*   (4.ie - p.45)
rye -   See *wry*   (6.y - p.46)
whys* - See *wise*   (1.i-e - p.42)
* A root with an inflection

6. y   (by, fly)

by -   Preposition - *We went home by way of the highway.* or *I went for a walk by the river.*

Also: **buy** - *That new car was a great **buy**, wasn't it?* or *Peggy went out **to buy** some new clothing.*
Also: **bye** - *He drew a **bye** in the tournament.* or *By the **bye** (incidentally), did you go to the party?*
pried* - (From **to pry** - See also **pride** 1.i-e - p.39)
pries* - (From **to pry** - See also **pride** 1.i-e - p.39)
rynd - See **rind** (2.i - 43)
whys* - See **wise** (1.i-e - p.46)
wry - *The man gave me a very **wry** (twisted or distasteful) look.* or *Bill has a very **wry** (ironic or humorous) sense of humor.*
Also: **rye** - *From the **rye** seed one can make bread or whiskey.* or *A gentleman among gypsies is referred to as a **rye**.*

* A root with an inflection

7. ei (height, sleight)

heigh -	See **hie**	(4.ie - p.44)
sleight -	See **slight**	(2.i - p.43)
speiss -	See **spice**	(1.i-e - p.40)

8. uy (buy, guy)

buy -	See **by**	(6.y - p.45)
guyed* -	See **guide**	(1.i-e - p.38)
guys* -	See **guise**	(i.i-e - p.38)

9. oi (choir)

choir -	See **quire**	(1.i-e - p.39)

10. eye (eye)

eye -	See **I**	(2.i - p.42)

11. aye (aye)

aye -	See **I**	(2.i - p.42)

VI - The Short Vowel Sound of I

Alphabetic Representation	Sound-symbol Representation	Number of Homonyms
1. i	in, it, slip	68
2. y	cyst, myth	9
3. i-e	give, live	0

Total - 77 Homonyms

1. i   (in, it, slip)

bib -   The baby wore a clean **bib** when she ate her cereal. or The men are going there **to bib** (to drink or imbibe).
  Also: **bibb** - A **bibb** is a bracket used on the mast of a ship.
bibb -   See **bib**   (1.i - p.47)
billed* - See **build**   (1.i - p.47)
bin -   The trucker put the load of coal into the **bin**. or Dad is going **to bin** the coal.
  Also: **been** [1] irregular past participle of to be - Have you **been** to see Lisa and Jessie yet? (See also **been**[2] - III [1.ee] p.21)
bit -   Can I have a little **bit** of soup? or His drill needed a new **bit** (a boring tool). or The horse's **bit** was loose. or A **bit** is a term used to describe a single character of language in a computer. or The rider will **bit** (put the bit in) the horse for you. or irregular past tense form to bite - The dog **bit** me.
  Also: **bitt** - A **bitt** is a vertical post on a ship's deck used to secure cables. or The sailor is going to **bitt** the cable.
bitt -   See **bit**   (1.i - p.47)
build - Arnold has a very athletic **build**. or Where is Dad going **to build** the new barn?
  Also: **billed** - past tense form of to bill - Was he **billed** for the entire amount?
cinque -   See **sink**   (1.i - p.51)

cist - *A cist was an ancient Roman wicker receptacle for carrying sacred objects.* or *Cist was the name used for a Neolithic stone coffin.*
  Also: *cyst* - *Mother had a small cyst* (a small sac or vesicle) *removed from her arm.*
fizz - *I saw some fizz in my glass.* or *The liquid will fizz when I add it to the glass.*
  Also: *phiz* - (Archaic Slang) *Phiz was a term once used for a face or a facial expression.*
gild - *The metalsmith will gild the cup with gold leaf.* or *Don't try to gild* (gloss over) *this situation.*
  Also: *guild* - *Does he belong to the artists guild?* or *A guild is a member of a small and specialized group of plants.*
gilt - *The frame of the painting was covered in gilt.* or *A gilt is a young sow who has not yet farrowed* (given birth). or alternate past tense form of *to gild* - *Has he gilt the cup yet?*
  Also: *guilt* - *The accused man was found to be without guilt.*
grill - *We cooked the steaks on the grill.* or *Dad is going to grill the hot dogs outside.*
  Also: *grille* - *A grille is a metal grating used as a screen, divider, or a decorative element in a door or gate.* (Variant spelling grill)
grille -   See *grill*   (1.i - p.48)
grip - *The grip on my bicycle was lost.* or *The boy fell when Jim lost his grip on his friend's hand.* or *Bill tried to grip the bar more tightly.*
  Also: *grippe* - *The doctor told me I had a case of the grippe* (influenza).
grippe - See *grip*   (1.i - p.48)
guild - See *gild*   (1.i - p.48)
guilt - See *gilt*   (1.i - p.48)
in - *A person in a position of influence or power is often referred to as an "in".* or (Preposition) *Jack went in the house.* or *We saw a bird in the tree.*
  Also: *inn* - *The family stayed at the old inn during the storm.*
inn -   See *in*   (1.i - p.48)

it's** - *it is* - See *its*   (1.i - p.49)
it's** - *it has* - See *its*   (1.i - p.49)
its -   possessive form of the pronoun *it* - *The rose has lost its petals.*
  Also: *it's* - contraction of *it is* - *It's too late to go to the game now.*
  Also: *it's* - contraction of *it has* - *It's gone past the filing date for this year.*
jinks* - See *jinx*   (1.i - p.49)
jinx - (Informal) *That boy is a jinx.* or *His prediction is going to jinx the team.*
  Also: *jinks* - plural form of *jink* - *The car made several jinks* (quick evasive turns) *to the left.* or *The boy on the bike jinks as he goes down the hill.*
kill - *The hunter shot the deer and got his kill.* or *A creek or stream is sometimes called a kill, especially in place names, as in Wallkill.* or *The object of the war seems to be only to kill the enemy.*
  Also: *kiln* [1] - *A kiln is an oven used to process materials for burning and hardening, such as grain or clay.* or *He used the new oven to kiln the bricks.* (In kiln[2] the final consonant **n** is pronounced)
kiln [1] - See *kill*   (1.i - p.49)
knit - *Her jacket had a beautiful knit.* or *Mother is going to knit gloves for each of us.*
  Also: *nit* - *A young louse, or the egg of a louse, is called a nit.*
limb - *The woodsman cut off a limb from the tree.* or *The jointed appendage of an animal, such as an arm, leg, wing, or flipper, is referred to as a limb.* or *The word limb is a term sometimes used in astronomy and botany.* or *The woodsman is going to limb the giant tree.*
  Also: *limn* - (Archaic) *The verb to limn meant to describe,* or *to depict, by painting or drawing.*
limn - See *limb*   (1.i - p.49)
lin -   *The lin is a name sometimes used for the linden tree.* (Also **linn**) or *A lin is a collection of water above*

49

or below a waterfall. (Also **linn**) or *A lin is also a name given to a waterfall.* (Also **linn** or **lyn**)
    Also: *Lynn is a large city in Massachusetts; Lynn is also a feminine given name*
linn -   See *lin*   (1.i - p.48)
links* - See *lynx*   (2.y - p.53)
mil -   See *mill*   (1.i - p.50)
mill - *The men work in the old cider mill.* or *I got a pepper mill for my birthday.* or *Do they grind flour in that mill?* or *The men are going to mill that material later.*
    Also: *mil - A mil is a unit of measurement; it is also the name of a coin used in Cyprus.*
minks* - See *minx*   (1.i - p.50)
minx - *Why is she such a minx* (pert or flirtatious)?
    Also: *minks* - a plural form of *mink* - *Bernice and I raised minks on the farm.* (Plural form also *mink*)
missed* - See *mist*   (1.i - p.50)
mist - *A light mist covered the ground with moisture.* or *The perfume came from its dispenser in a fine mist.* or *It is going to mist and all will be hidden from clear view.*
    Also: *missed* - past tense form of *to miss* - *The ball missed my head by an inch.*
nit -   See *knit*   (1.i - p.49)
phiz -   See *fizz*   (1.i - p.48)
picked* - See *Pict*   (1.i - p.50)
picks* - See *pyx*   (2.y - p.53)
Pict - *A Pict was one of the ancient people of North Britain.*
    Also: *picked* - past tense form of *to pick* - *Dad picked up his tools and left.*
pix* -   See *pyx*   (2.y - p.53)
prince - (Archaic) *A prince was a hereditary ruler.* or *The prince and princess went away.*
    Also: *prints* - plural form of *print* - *May I buy two of those prints?* or present tense form of *to print* - *The small boy prints his name carefully.*
prints* - See *prince* (1.i - p.50)
riffed* - See *rift*   (1.i - p.51)

rift - A *rift* is a narrow fissure in rock. or The backwash from a wave that has broken is called the *rift*. or Time will cause the rock formation to *rift*.
    Also: *riffed* - (Slang) past tense form of *to rif* - The old man was was *riffed* (dismissed from employment).

ring - John gave Mary a lovely *ring* for her birthday. or The boxer stepped into the *ring*. or He drew a *ring* around his drawing. or Why did he *ring* the bell?
    Also: **wring** - He bought a new maching to **wring** out his clothes more fully. or I am going to **wring** (twist) his neck for him. or The actor knows how to **wring** our emotions from us.

sic - The boy wanted to *sic* his police dog on the bully, but he didn't. or *Sic* is a Latin term meaning <u>thus</u> or <u>so</u>. (Also pronounced to rhyme with **seek**.)
    Also: **sick** - Dad was **sick**; Mom was sicker; but Tom was the sickest. or The **sick** dog couldn't eat.

sick - See *sic*   (1.i - p.51)

sink - She put too many dishes in the *sink*. or A cesspool is referred to sometimes as a *sink*. or The ocean liner began to *sink* below the surface of the sea. or His ambition will *sink* away to nothing if he loses this job. or His face began to *sink* into oblivion when he stopped making films.
    Also: **sync** (Informal) Are all our watches in **sync** (in synchronization)? or We had to **sync** our engines to get them timed properly.
    Also: **cinque** - **Cinque** is the number five in cards or dice.

stich - A *stich* is a line of verse.
    Also: **stitch** - The seamstress put a single **stitch** in the cloth. or The runner stopped because of a **stitch** (sharp pain) in his side. or Will he **stitch** my jacket for me.

stitch - See *stich*   (1.i - p.51)
sticks* - See *Styx*   (2.y - p.53)

tic   - A *tic* is a habitual spasmodic muscular contraction, or twitch, usually occurring in the face or the extremities.
        Also: *tick* - I heard the *tick* of the clock all night long. or A *tick* is a type of wingless parasite. or Mom bought a new *tick* (cloth case) for my pillow. or The clock began to *tick*. or The meter will *tick* off the fare as we drive home.

tick -   See *tic*   (1.i - p.52)
which -   See *witch*   (1.i - p.52)
Whig -   See *wig*   (1.i - p.52)
whit -   See *wit*   (1.i - p.52)

wig -   Where did the actress get her dark red *wig*. or (British Informal) The group members will *wig* (censure) the old man.
       Also: *Whig* - A *Whig* was a political party in the 18th and 19th centuries which was opposed to the Tories. (Properly pronounced *hwig*)

win - This victory was a big *win* for the team. or Our club is going to *win* a trophy.
       Also: A *wynn* is a kind of timber truck or carriage.

wind - I can hear the *wind* blowing through the trees. or The boss just told me that something important is in the *wind*.
       Also: (Scottish) A *wynd* is a narrow lane or alley.

wit -   The teacher was well known for his *wit*.
       Also: *whit* - I don't care a *whit* (the least bit) about your opinion. (Properly pronounced *hwit*)

witch - Did you see that *witch* go flying by on a broomstick? or The wicked woman in the story tried to *witch* (cast a spell over) the children.
       Also: *which* - pronoun - *Which* of these is yours? or relative pronoun - You can stay in this room, *which* is small. or *Which* part of the book did you like? (Properly pronounced *hwich*)

with - (Preposition) Dad came home *with* the groceries.
       Also: *withe* - A *withe* is a tough, supple twig. or She tried to *withe* the sticks with a willow twig.

withe -   See *with*   (1.i - p.52)
wring -   See *ring*   (1.i - p.51)

* A root with an inflection
** A contraction

2. y   cyst, myth

cyst -   See *cist*   (1.i - p.48)
lyn -   See *lin*   (1.i - p.49)
Lynn -   See *lin*   (1.i - p.49)
lynx -   A *lynx* is a kind of wild cat.
    Also: *links* - plural form of *link* - The chain has ten *links* in it. or Are there bridge *links* into the city? or This chain *links* the gates together.
pyx -   The priest placed the sacred wafers into his *pyx* (a container for holding sacred objects). or While coins are awaiting valuation in a mint, they are placed in a chest called a *pyx*. (Also **pix**)
    Also: *picks* - plural form of *pick* - Do I get more than two *picks*? or present tense form of to pick - The small boy *picks* up his toys and puts them away.
    Also: *pix* - (Slang) I want to see the *pix* (motion pictures or photographs).
Styx* -   In Greek Mythology, the river *Styx* is one of the rivers of Hades.
    Also: *sticks* - plural form of *stick* - The little boy collected a pile of *sticks*. or a present tense form of to stick - Dad tried to *stick* some rags into the hole to keep out the wind.
sync -   See *sink*   (1.i - p.51)
wynn -   See *win*   (1.i - p.52)
wynd -   See *wind*   (1.i - p.52)

3. i-e (give, live)

Note: There are no homonyms able to be found for this very rare sound-symbol category.

V - The Long Vowel Sound of O

Alphabetic Representation	Sound-symbol Representation	Number of Homonyms
1. o-e	cone, hole	43
2. o	cold, so,	20
3. oa	boat, oak,	20
4. oe	doe, toe	11
5. ow*	bowl, tow	22
6. ou	dough, soul	4
7. oh	oh	2
8. ew	sew	1
9. owe	owe	1
10. eau	beau	1

Total - 125 Homonyms

* The numerical placement for #5 is in error and will be corrected in the next edition. It should be #2.

1. o-e   (cone, hole)

bode - *His attitude does not **bode*** (portend) *well for the future.*
    Also: ***bowed*** - past tense form of *to bow* - *He **bowed** the wood into the shape he desired.* or *The musician **bowed** his cello to produce a lovely sound.*

bole - *I sat on the **bole*** (trunk) *of the old tree..*
    Also: ***bowl*** - *Mom put my soup into a blue **bowl**.* or *The new football stadium was in the shape of a **bowl**.* or *Did you have a **bowl** yet?* or *We went to **bowl** at the new bowling lanes.* or *In cricket, the one has to **bowl*** (hurl) *the ball toward the batsman.*
    Also: ***boll*** - *The **boll** is the rounded seed pod of certain plants, and the **boll** weevil is a beetle that attacks the **boll** of the cotton plant.*

bore - See ***boar***   XVIIA   (2. oar - p.95)

close - *I had to close the door to keep out the snow.* or *Darkness began to close in on us.*

Also: *clothes* - only used in plural form

Note: Although this form of the noun is not a homonym of *close*, it is an example of a "sound misperception," one which causes a serious problem for poor spellers. It appears here only to help those who hear these two words as being the same, whatever the initial cause of such confusion may be. It usually is misheard in sentences such as, *Put your clothes away.* or *He got new clothes for his birthday.* It is properly pronounced as though it were spelled as - clothze, and not as cloze.

clothes* -   See *close*   (1.o-e - p.55)
cokes* -   See *coax*   (2.oa - p.62)
cole - (Rare)*The cole is a plant, such as the cabbage, and is also called "colewort."*

Also: *coal* - *Coal is a dark brown to black fossil-derived material used as fuel.* or *All that was left of the fire was a single coal.* or *The stoker had to coal up the fire.*

core - See XVIIA   (3.ore - p.97)
cote - *Birds and sheep sometimes live in a shelter called a cote.*

Also: *coat* - *Why don't you ever wear your warm coat?* or *The old house needs a coat of paint.* or *When are you going to coat the shoes with a protective coating?*

doze -   *Dad took a little doze on the couch.* or *My old dog likes to doze in the sun.*

Also: *does* - plural form of *doe* - *All the does (female deer) were in the field.*
(Alternate plural spelling - *doe*)

fore - See XVIIA   (3.ore - p.97)
gnome - *A gnome was a dwarflike creature in fables who lived underground and guarded treasures.* or *The shriveled old man is sometimes referred to as a gnome.*

Also: **nome** - A **nome** is a name for an ancient Egyptian province, or a modern Greek one.
Also: **Nome** - **Nome** is a city in Alaska.

hole - Is that a **hole** I see in your sweater? or I see a small **hole** in the clouds. or They dug a huge **hole** in the ground. or The shoemaker is going to **hole** the piece of leather. or He had to **hole** out to win the golf match.
Also: The sum of the parts is greater than the **whole**. or Why did Jim eat the **whole** pie?

holed* - See **hold**   (2.o - p.60)

hose - Use the **hose** and water the lawn. or They bought some **hose** (socks or stockings) at the store. or The firemen had to **hose** down the fire for a long time.
Also: **hoes** - plural form of hoe - Jack bought five new **hoes**. or a present tense form of to hoe - The man **hoes** a field.

lode - A **lode** is a fissure in rock filled with metal ore. or This ore came from a rich **lode**.
Also: **load** - The farmer will bring a **load** of hay. or Can you help to **load** the crates into the truck?
Also: **lowed** - past tense form of to low - The cattle **lowed** in the fields.

lone - He painted the **lone** tree on the hillside.
Also: **loan** - Can I get a **loan** from the bank? or Tom is going to **loan** me some books.

mode - He followed an ancient **mode** in his glass blowing. or She dressed in the latest **mode** (style). or The word **mode** is one used in physics, logic, geology, music, and statistics.
Also: **mowed** - past tense form of to mow - Dad **mowed** the field with his tractor.

mote - His role was but a **mote** (speck) in the total plan.
Also: **moat** - The town wanted a deep **moat** (ditch) dug around the town to protect it. or The king told his soldiers to **moat** the castle and fill it with water.

nome - See **gnome**   (1. o-e - p.55)
Nome - See **gnome**   (1. o-e - p.56)

nose - *He hurt his **nose** when he fell down.* or *The **nose** of the plane was damaged.* or *The dog can **nose** out drugs in luggage.* or *My horse is going to **nose** out yours in this race.*
    Also: ***knows*** - present tense form of *to know* - *The small child **knows** right from wrong.*
    Also: ***nos*** - plural form of *no* - *I won the election, three yeses to two **nos**.*

ode - *An **ode** is a long lyrical poem, usually rhymed, and often delivered to a praised person or object; it was also a poetic form used in classical literature.*
    Also: ***owed*** - past tense form of *to owe* - *Jim **owed** the bank a great deal of money.*

pole - *How does he climb that **pole** so fast?* or *A **pole** is a region which is an axial extremity of any axis through a sphere.* or *A **pole** may be either of two opposing ideas or forces.* or *We had to **pole** the boat through the shallow water.*
    Also: ***poll*** - *We had a **poll** to see who would be elected.* or *They decided to have a public opinion **poll** to see who was most popular.* or *They had to **poll** all the members of the club.*

pome - *A **pome** is a fleshy fruit having seeds but no stone, such as an apple or a pear.*
    Also: ***poem*** - Although this word is properly pronounced in two syllables - **po' em**, it is frequently misperceived and pronouned as though it rhymed with **pome**, especially by those whose spelling development has been disrupted by faulty instruction or poor speech models.

prose - ***Prose** is ordinary speech or writing, as distinguished from verse.* or *I think I will **prose** (write prose) this material.*
    Also: ***pros*** - plural form of *pro* - *The **pros** argued against the cons.* or (Informal) *Those players aren't amateurs, they're **pros** (professionals).*

rode - irregular past tense form of *to ride* - *Yesterday the gang **rode** into town and robbed the bank.*

Also: **road** - *The work crew came out to repair the old road.* or *The actors went on the road once again.*

Also: **rowed** [1] - past tense form of *to row* - *We all cheered as the team rowed by.*

role - *Jane played the role of the judge in the new play.* or *Parents play an important role in children's development.*

Also: **roll** - *I got a plain roll from the bakery.* or *The gambler had a roll of bills that would choke a horse.* or *I heard the roll of the drums.* or *The child likes to roll down the hill.* or *He can roll himself up into a tiny ball.*

Rome - *The capital city of Italy is Rome.*

Also: **roam** - *I like to roam around without a plan when I'm on vacation.*

rose - *Would you like a red rose from my garden?* or irregular past tense form of *to rise* - *The plane rose slowly from the ground.*

Also: **rows** [1] - plural form of *row* - *We sat ten rows behind you.* or present tense form of *to row* - *Bill rows the boat across the lake.*

rote - *He learned to spell by rote* (repetitious memorization). or *A rote was a medieval stringed instrument.* or *He had a good rote memory.*

Also: **wrote** - irregular past tense form of *to write* - *Last week he wrote his name on the wall.*

soke - *In early English law, a soke was a feudal right of lordship.*

Also: **soak** - *Mom said to give the clothes a good soak before washing them.* or *She also said to soak them in a strong bleach.* or *Why do some people try to soak* (overcharge) *unsuspecting visitors?*

sole - *I had a new sole put on my shoe.* or *The small child was the sole* (only) *survivor of the plane crash.* or *The sole is a flatfish which is valued as a food fish.* or *He is going to sole my shoes for me. The golfer will sole his club before hitting the ball.*

Also: **soul** - *The* **soul** *has long been thought to be the animating principle underlying human life.* or *That poor* **soul** *lost all his savings in the fire.*
soled* - See **sold** (2.o - p.61)
sone - *A* **sone** *is a subjective unit of loudness.*
   Also: **sewn** - an irregular past tense form of *to sew* - *The dress was* **sewn** *by an expert seamstress.*
   Also: **sown** - irregular past tense form of *to sow* - *The seeds were* **sown** *by the farmer.*
sore - See **soar** XVIIA (2.oar - p.97)
throne - *The king sat on his* **throne** *and spoke to his people.* or *The power of the* **throne** *is great.* or *They are going* **to throne** (to enthrone, or place upon the throne) *the new king and queen.*
   Also: **thrown** - irregular past participle form of *to throw* - *Why was the box* **thrown** *from the truck?*
tole - **Tole** *was a kind of 18th century laquered or enameled metalware.*
   Also: **toll** - *A* **toll** *is a fee charged for an access or a privelege, such as crossing a bridge or shipping goods over long distances.*
tore - See **tor** XVIIA (1.or - p.95)
whole - See **hole** (1.o-e)
whore - See **hoar** XVIIA (2.oar - p.96)
whored* - See XVIIA (or)
wrote - See **rote** (1.o-e - p.58)
yoke - *A new* **yoke** *encircled the necks of the oxen.* or *A* **yoke** *is also a kind of clamp or vise used to hold parts together.* or *The farmer was going* **to yoke** *them together.*
   Also: **yolk** - *The* **yolk** *is the yellow mass of egg which is surrounded by albumen; it is also a substance found in unprocessed sheep's wool.*

* A root with an inflection

2. **o**   (cold, so)

bo - (Slang) *The word* **bo** *is a word used to describe a pal or a fellow, probably a shortened form of Hobo or Bozo.*

Also: **bow** - *The car came to a **bow** (bend or curve) in the road.* or *The archer aimed his **bow** at the animal.* or *The **bow** of my eyeglasses is broken.* or *The carpenter tried to **bow** the wood.* or *The violinist likes to **bow** his violin.*

Also: **beau** - *A **beau** is the sweetheart of a woman or girl; it is also a name used to describe a man overly interested in clothing or social etiquette.*

bold - *His actions in the battle were very **bold**.*

Also: **bowled** - *The bowlers **bowled** all night long.*

boll - See **bole** (1.o-e - p.54)

cold - *My mother has a bad **cold**.* or *She can't stand the **cold**.* or *My auto engine was **cold** this morning.* or *He didn't jump because he got **cold** feet* (became frightened). or *His **cold** logic overpowered us.* or *She gave him the **cold** shoulder.*

Also: **coaled** - past tense form of *to coal* - *Have the fires been **coaled** yet?*

do - See **doe** (4. oe - p.62)

fold - *The paper had a **fold** in it.* or *Are you going tto **fold** the clothes for me now?*

Also: **foaled** - past tense form of *to foal* - *The mare **foaled** (gave birth) last night.*

ho - (Interjection) *The captain shouted, "Land **ho**!"*

Also: **hoe** - *She gave me a **hoe** and asked me to dig up some weeds.* or *I went out to **hoe** in the garden.*

hold - *The seamen loaded the cargo in the **hold**.* or *The robber had a **hold** on my neck.* or *Can you put a **hold** on my mail for a few days?* or *I had to **hold** on for dear life.* or *I think I can **hold** on to it now.*

Also: **holed** - past tense form of *to hole* - *The shoemaker **holed** the leather.* or *He won the golf match when he **holed** out.* or *The crooks were **holed** up in the small shack.*

mot - *A **mot** is a clever saying or a witticism.*

Also: **mow** - *A **mow** is a place for storing hay or grain.* or *Dad asked me to **mow** the lawn.* or *The machine gun is a weapon that can **mow** down many soldiers at a time.*

no - *I have **no** food for you.* or *I said **no**; he said yes.*
    Also: ***know*** - *The gambler won because he was in the **know**.* or *I want to **know** the entire truth at once.*
    Also: ***Noh*** - ***Noh** is a specialized form of classical Japanese drama, which is performed in a very stylized manner and accompanied by music and dance.* (Also spelled in lower case as **noh**, and as **no**.)

nos* -	See ***nose***	(1.o-e - p.57)
poll -	See ***pole***	(1.o-e - p.57)
pros* -	See ***prose***	(1.o-e - p.57)
roll -	See ***role***	(1.o-e - p.58)

so - *I told him **so**.* or *He was my friend and he remained **so** for many years.* or *He was late and **so** was I.*
    Also: ***sow***[1] - *The farmer went out to **sow** seeds in his field.*
    Also: ***sew*** - *Where did mother learn to **sew** so well?*

sold - *irregular* past tense form of *to sell* - *When was the property **sold**?*
    Also: ***soled*** - past tense form of *to sole* - *When were his shoes **soled**?*

told - irregular past tense form of *to tell* - *The boy was **told** of his test failure.*
    Also: ***tolled*** - past tense form of *to toll* - *As the bells **tolled**, the people left the church.*

toll -	See ***tole***	(1. o-e - 59)
tolled* -	See ***told***	(2. o - p.61)
yolk -	See ***yoke***	(1. o-e - p.59)

* A root with an inflection

3. oa   oak, boat

boar -	See **XVIIA**	(2. oar - p.95)
board -	See **XVIIA**	(2. oar - p.95)
coal -	See ***cole***	(1. o-e - p.55)
coaled* -	See ***cold***	(2. o - p.60)
coarse -	See **XVIIA**	(2. oar - p.96)

coat - See *cote*   (1. o-e - p.55)
coax - Mother can *coax* the baby to eat her food easily.
       Also: *cokes* - plural form of *coke* - *Cokes* are residues obtained from coal by distillation. <u>or</u> The worker *cokes* (converts) the fuel.
foaled* - See *fold*   (2. o - p.60)
groan - Did you hear a *groan* coming from the closet? <u>or</u> He didn't want to *groan* about his injuries.
       Also: *grown* - irregular past participle form of *to grow* - He has *grown* into a fine looking dog. <u>or</u> The child must be full-*grown* by now.
hoar -   See **XVIIA**   (2. oar - p.96)
hoard -   See **XVIIA**   (2. oar - p.96)
load -   See *lode*   (1. o-e - p.56)
loan -   See *lone*   (1. o-e - p.56)
moan - I heard a *moan* coming from the room. <u>or</u> The old man likes to *moan* to get attention.
       Also: *mown* - alternate past tense form of *to mow* - All the hay was *mown* by evening. <u>or</u> All the *mown* hay was baled.
moat -   See *mote*   (1. o-e - p.56)
road -   See *rode*   (1. o-e - p.57)
roam -   See *Rome*   (1. o-e - p.58)
soak -   See *soke*   (1. o-e - p.58)
soar -   See **XVIIA**   (2. oar - p.97)
toad - A tailess amphibian, or a type of lizard, can be referred to as a *toad*. <u>or</u> I think you're a *toad* (repulsive person).
       Also: *towed* - past tense form of *to tow* - Last night my car was *towed* from the accident.
       Also: *toed* - He *toed* nail into the wood at an angle. <u>or</u> I saw a two-*toed* sloth at the zoo.
whoa - See *woe*   (4. oe - p.64)
* A root with an inflection

4. oe   (doe, toe)

doe - A *doe* is the name for a female deer, also a number of related animals, such as the hare and the kangaroo.(The plural forms are either *does* or *doe*)

        Also: ***dough*** - *The **dough** that the baker uses for bread and rolls is very moist.* or (Slang) *He needs some **dough** (money) in a hurry.*
        Also: ***do*** - *The first tone of the diatonic scale in solfegio is **do**, as in do-re-mi, etc.*
does*** - See ***doze***   (1. o-e - p.63)
floe - *The large **floe** of ice drifted aimlessly in the ocean.*
        Also: ***flow*** - *The **flow** of the water was rapid.* or *There was a great **flow** of ideas coming from the class.* or *Where does the river **flow** into the sea?*
hoe - See ***ho***   (2. o - p.60)
hoes*** - See ***hose***   (1. o-e - p.63)
roe - ***Roe*** *is both the egg laden ovary of a fish, and the egg mass found in certain crustaceans.*
        Also: ***row*** [1] - *My friend sat in the **row** of seats just behind me.* or *I live in that **row** of houses.* or *We took a **row** up the stream.* or *Can you please **row** this boat faster?*
sloe - *The **sloe** is a plant in the blackthorn family.* or *To be **sloe** eyed is to have soft, slanted, dark eyes.*
        Also: ***slow*** - *Father tried to **slow** down the car.* or *One cannot stop the **slow** and inexorable march of time.* or *Tom is a very **slow** runner.* or *Jim is a **slow** learner.*
throe - *The expectant mother said she felt a **throe*** (spasm of pain) *every ten minutes.* (Often used in the plural, as "*in the throes of childbirth*")
        Also: ***throw*** - *That was a good **throw** Sam.* or *The pitcher tried to **throw** a fast ball, but couldn't.*
toe - *I hurt my big **toe** when I walked into the chair.* or *I like to **toe** the sand and feel its wetness.* or *I had to **toe*** (hit obliquely) *the nail to hold the board in place.* or *If you don't **toe** the mark, you'll be disqualified.*
        Also: ***tow*** - ***Tow*** *is coarse broken hemp fiber prepared for spinning.* or *Can you please give me a **tow** to the garage?* or *The truck will **tow** my ruined auto to the shop for repair.* or *Is the **tow** truck coming soon?*
toed*** - See ***toad***   (3.oa - p.62)

woe - *Woe* (misfortune) *to the man who enters these doors.*
Also: *whoa* - (Interjection) *Whoa!* (A command to a horse to stop - properly pronounced as *hwoe*.)
* A root with an inflection

5. o w   (bowl, tow)

bow -	See *bo*	(2. o - p.59)
bowed* -	See *bode*	(1. o-e - p.54)
bowl -	See *bole*	(1. o-e - p.54)
bowled* -	See *bold*	(2. o - p.60)
flow -	See *floe*	(4. oe - p.63)
grown -	See *groan*	(3. oa - p.62)
know -	See *no*	(2. o - p.61)
knows* -	See *nose*	(1. o-e - p.57)
lowed* -	See *lode*	(1. o-e - p.56)
mow -	See *mot*	(2. o - p.60)
mowed* -	See *mode*	(1. o-e - p.56)
mown -	See *moan*	(3. oa - p.62)
owed* -	See *ode*	(1. o-e - p.57)
row [1] -	See *roe*	(4. oe - p.63)
rowed [1]* -	See *rode*	(1. o-e - p.57)
rows [1]* -	See *rose*	(1. o-e - p.58)
slow -	See *sloe*	(4. oe - p.63)
sow [1] -	See *so*	(2. o - p.61)
sown -	See *sone*	(1. o-e - p.64)
throw -	See *throe*	(4. oe - p.63)
thrown -	See *throne*	(1. o-e - p.59)
tow -	See *toe*	(4. oe - p.63)
towed* -	See *toad*	(2. oa - p.62)

* A root with an inflection

6. o u   (dough, soul)

course -	See *coarse* XVIIA	(2. oar - p.96)
dough -	See *doe*	(4. oe - p.62)
four -	See *fore* XVIIA	(3. ore - p.97)
soul -	See *sole*	(1. o-e p.58)

7. oh   (oh)

oh -   (Interjection) ***Oh!*** *What are you doing here?*
         Also: ***owe*** *- I **owe** him a great deal of money.* or
         *Why do you think I **owe** you an apology?*
noh - See ***no***   (2.o   - p.65)

8. ew   (sew)

sew -   See ***so***   (2.o   - p.61)
sewn - See ***sone***   (1.o-e - p.59)

9. owe   (owe)

owe -   See ***oh***   (7.oh - p.65)

10. eau   (beau)

beau - See ***bo***   (2.o   - p.59)

VII - The Short Vowel Sound of O

Alphabetic Representation	Sound-symbol Representation	Number of Homonyms
1. o	odd, stop,	28
2. a	watt, what	7

Total - 35 Homonyms

1. o   (odd, stop)

bloc - *The whole group voted as a solid **bloc**.*
         Also: ***block*** *- The building took up a city **block***. or
         *The child threw a toy **block** out the window.* or
         *The safe was lifted by a **block** and tackle.* or
         (Slang) *I'm going to knock your **block** off.* or

*Don't try to **block** the path ever again.* or *We will **block** the load to support it.*
block - See **bloc**   (1.o - p.65)
bomb - *The plane dropped dropped a **bomb** on the fort.* or (Slang) *The quarterback threw a long **bomb** for a touchdown.* or (Slang) *That play was a real **bomb**.* or *The air force decided to **bomb** the city.*
   Also: **bombe** - *A **bombe** is a frozen dessert containing several layers of different flavors of ice cream.*
bombe - See **bomb**   (1.o - p.66)
cocks* - See **cox**   (1.o - p.66)
conch[1] - *A **conch** is a marine mollusk having a spiral shell and edible flesh.* (Also **conch**[2] pronounced to rhyme with **ponch**.)
   Also: **conk** - *Conk is a kind of fungus.* or (Slang) *A **conk** may be the head, the nose, or a blow.* or (Slang) *Dave tried to **conk** me on the head.* or (Slang) *The engine started to **conk** out.*
conk - See **conch**   (1.o - p.66)
cops* - See **copse**   (1.o - p.66)
copse - *We stood together in a **copse** (a thicket of trees).*
   Also: **cops** - (Informal) *The **cops** (policemen) were at the scene of the crime.*
copped* - See **Copt**   (1.o - p.66)
Copt - *A **Copt** is a native of Egypt descended from ancient Egyptian stock.*
   Also: **copped** - (Informal) - past tense form of *to cop* - *The thief **copped** (stole) a ring from the store.*
cox - (Informal) *Jack was the **cox** (coxswain) for our boat.*
   Also: **cocks** - plural form of *cock* - *The **cocks** (a rooster or a male bird) were in the yard.* or *Both **cocks** (parts of a faucet) were broken.* or present tense form of *to cock* - *The policeman **cocks** his revolver.*
flocks* - See **phlox**   (1.o - p.67)
knob - *The **knob** on the door wouldn't turn.* or *We climbed the **knob** of the hill.*

Also: **nob** - (Slang) - *He hit his **nob** (head) on the door.* or *That man acts like a **nob*** (a person of wealth or social standing).
knock - *Did you hear a **knock** at the door?* or *He is about to **knock** on the door.*
   Also: **nock** - *The **nock** is the groove at the end of the bow for attaching the bowstring.* or *He is going to **nock** (notch) the bow now.*
knot - *Dad tied a **knot** in my shoe lace.* or *All the men stood together in a small **knot**.* or *Try not to **knot** the rope.*
   Also: **not** - *I will **not** go with you.* or *You may **not** have any more.*
locks* - See **lox**   (1.o - p.67)
lox - *I ate some **lox** (smoked salmon) on a bagel.* or ***Lox** is a form of liquid oxygen.*
   Also: **locks** - plural form of *lock* - *The **locks** on the doors were all broken.* or present tense form of *to lock* - *Danny **locks** the car door.*
nob -   See **knob**   (1.o - p.66)
nock -   See **knock**   (1.o - p.67)
not -   See **knot**   (1.o - p.67)
phlox - *The **phlox** is a North American plant with lance-shaped leaves and clusters of colored flowers.*
   Also: **flocks** - plural form of *flock* - *I saw seven **flocks** of geese flying south today.* or a present tense form of *to flock* - *The crowd **flocks** to see the results of the plane crash.* or *The worker **flocks** (stuffs with flock, which is made up of tufts of fiber, hair, or waste wool) the mattress.*
pocks* - See **pox**   (1.o - p.67)
pox - *Any disease which is characterized by purulent skin eruptions is referred to as a **pox**, such as chicken **pox** or small **pox**.*
   Also: **pocks** - plural form of *pock* - *Pustules, or scars, caused by smallpox are called **pocks**.*
shot   See **shott**   (1.o - p.67)
shott - *A **shott** is a depression surrounding a salt marsh.*
   (Variant spelling of **chott**)

Also: *shot* - *The hunter loaded shot into his shotgun.* or *I heard a shot fired from the hill.* or (Informal) *He is a good shot.* or *Tom had to shot* (load with shot) *the gun.* or irregular past tense form of *to shoot* - *The victim was shot in the arm.*

whop - *A whop is the sound of a sharp thud.* or *Dad wanted to whop the thief.* (Properly pronounced as hwop - See *whale* (I - 1.a-e - p.7)

Also: *wop* - The term *wop* is used derogatorily for an Italian. Its origin is thought to derive from a stamp used by US immigration authorities who marked the files of those with inadequate entry papers as "persons with out papers," or **WOP**.

wop - See *whop* (1.o - p.68)

* A root with an inflection

2. a   (wand, watt)

pa - (Informal) *Pa* (father or papa) *went to the store.*

Also: *pah* (Interjection) *Pah!* (an exclamation of disgust or irritation) *I can't stand it any longer.*

Also: *pas* (Ballet) *A pas is a dance step, or a series of steps.*

pah -   See *pa*   (2.a - p.68)
pas -   See *pa*   (2.a - p.68)
wand - *The magician used his wand when he did tricks.* or *Why does the mayor carry a wand when he's in a procession?* or *A wand is a thin and supple twig or stick.*

Also: *wanned* - (Poetic) past tense form of *to wan* - *When I was sentenced, I began to wan* (to pale).

wanned* - See *wand*   (2.a - p.68)
watt - *A watt is a unit of electric power.*

Also: *what* - *What time is it?* or *I'm going to the game, come what may.* or *Do you know what school you will attend?* (wh properly pronounced as *hw*) See *whale* (a-e)

what -   See *watt*   (2.a - p.68)

68

IX - The Long Vowel Sound of U

Alphabetic Representation	Sound-symbol Representation	Number of Homonyms
1. u-e	use, mule	2
2. ue	cue, hue	2
3. ew	yew	4
4. ewe	ewe	1
5. ueue	queue	1
6. you	you	1

Total - 11 Homonyms

Note: See also **XI (OO)**

1. **u-e**   (use, mule)

mule - *The stubborn old **mule** wouldn't move.* or (Informal) *Sometimes my brother acts like a **mule**.*
   Also: *mewl* - *The sick baby made a weak **mewl*** (cry). or *All the ailing puppy can do now is to **mewl** weakly.*

muse - *In my **muse**, I had some deep thoughts.* or *In Greek Mythology, a **Muse** was one of the nine daughters of Mnemosyne and Zeus.* or *The poet will **muse** over his thoughts before he writes a poem.*
   Also: *mews* - plural form of *mew* - *The baby's cries sounded like a cat's **mews**.* or *The old man walked through the **mews*** (a secret or secluded place) *to get to his house.* or ***Mews** can also be a kind of sea bird, or cages for hawks.* or present tense form of *to mew* - *The cat **mews** for attention.*

2. **ue**   (cue, hue)

cue - *The actor missed his **cue**.* or *The psychologist looked for a **cue** to explain her behavior.* or *When we speak to the boss, you take your **cue** from me.* or

> *Why did he place his **cue** on the table after he hit the pool ball.* or *The director tried to **cue** the stumbling actor.* or *Try to **cue** the ball more accurately next time.*
>> Also: **queue** - *There was a long **queue** for the new film.* or *He wore his hair in a braid, like a pigtail or a **queue**.* or *I am going to **queue** up before the line gets too long.*

hue - *The drapes were done in a colorful **hue**.* or *The actor projected a dangerous **hue** in his characterization.* or *They heard a terribly loud **hue** and cry.*
>> Also: **hew** - *The woodsman is going to **hew** the log into a canoe for me.* or *Why did they have to **hew** the old oak?*

3. ew   (yew)

hew - See **hue**   (2.ue - p.70)
mewl - See **mule**   (1.u-e - p.69)
mews* - See **muse**   (1.u-e - p.69)
yew - *A **yew** tree is an evergreen which often has poisonous scarlet berries.*
>> Also: **ewe** - *A **ewe** is a full grown female sheep.*
>> Also: **you** - the second person singular and plural pronoun form for the nominative and objective cases - ***You** are late again.* or *Did the ball hit **you** on the head?*

* A root with an inflection

4. ewe   (ewe)

ewe - See **yew**   (3.ew - p.70)

5. ueue   (queue)

queue - See **cue**   (2.ue - p.69)

6. you   (you)

you - See **yew**   (3.ew - p.70)

X - The Short Vowel Sound of U

Alphabetic Representation	Sound-symbol Representation	Number of Homonyms
1. u	rug, stub, us	28
2. o-e	come, some	5
3. o	son, ton, won	3
4. ou	rough, tough	2

Total - 38 Homonyms

1. **u**   (rug, stub, us)

bus -   *The bus was late and we missed the game.* or *The waiter put the dishes on a bus and wheeled them away.* or *Why did they have to bus the children to the new school?*
   Also: **buss** - (Regional) *He gave his wife a big buss* (a smacking kiss). or (Regional) *The man wanted to buss his wife at the party.*
buss -   See **bus**   (1.u - p.71)
bussed* - See **bust**   (1.u - p.71)
bust - *A woman's bosom is also called her bust.* or *A piece of sculpture representing the head, shoulders, and upper chest, is called a bust.* or (Slang) *Our business went bust.* or *I'm going to bust his jaw.* or *The gambler wants to bust the bank.*
   Also: **bussed** - past tense form of *to buss* - *He bussed* (kissed with a loud smacking sound) *his wife because he was so happy.*
   Also: **bused** - past tense form of *to bus* - *The children were bused* (driven by bus) *to school each day.* (Variant spelling - **bussed**)
but -   See **butt**   (1.u - p.71)
butt - *The angry ram gave me a butt with its horns.* or *The builder put a butt in the board to hold it fast.* or *The rifle butt is cracked.* or *Bob is always the butt of jokes.* or (Informal) *He kicked me in the*

butt (the buttocks) *The ram is going to butt me again.* or *That pest is going to butt in once again.* or *The carpenter will butt this joint here.*
    Also: **but** - (Conjunction) *You can go, but Jack must stay here.* or *All but Bill came home.* or *But for a bit of luck, I might have been in that wreck.*

cum - This preposition means "together with, or plus," as in "*my garage-cum-workshop.*"
    Also: **come** - *When will Dad come home?*

ducked* - See **duct**   (1.u - p.72)

duct - *Hot air was flowing through the duct.* or *Tears flow into the eye through a duct.*
    Also: **ducked** - past tense form of *to duck* - *Jim had to duck his head as he went through the door.*

dun - *The bill collector tried to dun the man for payment.*
    Also: **done** - irregular past participle of *to do* - *Why haven't you done your homework yet?*

mussed* - See **must** (1.u - p.72)

must - an auxiliary verb - *You must always obey your parents.* or *To each man death must come.*
    Also: **mussed** - past tense form of *to muss* - *The wind mussed up the girl's hair.*

nun - *The nun walked the children to the church.* or *A nun is also a type of bird.*
    Also: **none** -(Pronoun) *I have none, not one.*

plum - *I picked a ripe plum from the tree.* or *My new job was quite a plum.*
    Also: **plumb** - *A plumb is a suspended weight used to determine the water's depth.* or *He used a plumb to determine the true vertical.* or *The men on the ship are going to plumb the ocean's depth.* or *The lawyer tried to plumb the significance of the events.*

plumb - See **plum**   (1.u - p.72)

ruff - *A ruff was a circular starched, frilled, collar worn by men and women in the 16th and 17th centuries.* or *A ruff is either a card game itself, like whist, or a strategy use in a card game.* or *I lost because I didn't ruff* (play a trump card).

Also: **rough** - *I want you to cut the **rough** because the weeds are so high.* or *He had to **rough** up the edges so the glue would stick.* or *Our team is going to **rough** up our opponents.* or *On the camping trip, we had to **rough** it.* or *Will you file off the **rough** edge please?*

rhumb - *A **rhumb** is a point on a mariner's compass.*
    Also: **rum** - *We drank **rum** from a tall glass.* or (British Slang) *We were caught in a **rum** (queer or odd) situation.*

rum - See **rhumb** (1.u - p.73)

rung - *The first **rung** of my ladder is broken.* or *Can you replace a **rung** on this old chair?* or irregular past tense form of *to ring*, as in *to ring a bell* - *Was the bell **rung** by you?*
    Also: irregular past tense form of *to wring* - *Have you **wrung** out the clothes yet?* or *The police **wrung** a confession out of the thief.*

scull - *A **scull** is either a long oar twisted from side to side at the stern of a boat to propel it, a pair of short handled oars used by a single rower, or a small light racing boat.* or *I am going to **scull** this afternoon.*
    Also: **skull** - *The human brain is encased in a **skull**.* or *The student wore a **skull** cap in school.*

skull - See **scull** (1.u - p.73)

sum - *The **sum** of two plus two is four.* or *The **sum** of man's knowledge can be found in the written word.* or *Dad paid a large **sum** for his new car.* or *I am going to **sum** up what I have said now.*
    Also: **some** - *May I have **some** candy?* or *Some foolish person did this.* or as a pronoun *Some will and **some** won't.* or (Informal) *She is **some** dancer.*

sun - *The **sun** was shining high in the sky.* or *The **sun** is a star.* or *Where are you going to **sun** yourself, Peggy?*
    Also: **son** - *A **son** is a male offspring.* or *The young man was just like a **son** to me.*

trussed* - See **trust** (1.u - p.74)

trust - *I placed my trust in their decision.* or *The money was placed in the bank in trust for my future.* or *I want to trust you but I can't.* or *I trust that the train will arrive on time.*
    Also: *trussed* - past tense form of *to truss* - *The dead animal was trussed* (tied) *up before it was roasted.*
tuff - *Tuff is a kind of rock composed of volcanic ash.*
    Also: *tough* - (Informal) *The young tough was arrested by the police.* or *An elephant has a tough hide.*
tun - *A tun is a large cask, usually for wine.* or *A tun is also a measure of liquid capacity.*
    Also: *ton* - *A ton is a unit of weight measurement.* or *That box felt like it weighed a ton.*
wrung - See *rung*   (1.u - p.73)
* A root with an inflection

2. o-e   (come, some)

come - See *cum*   (1.u - p.72)
done - See *dun*   (1.u - p.72)
none - See *nun*   (1.u - p.72)
one - See *won*   (3.o - p.74)
some - See *sum*   (1.u - p.73)

3. o   (son, ton, won)

son - See *sun*   (1.u - p.73)
ton - See *tun*   (1.u - p.74
won - irregular past tense form of *to win* - *Who won the big game last night?*
    Also: *one* - *I had one and only one glass of water yesterday.*
    Note: The word *one* is unique, since there is no other extant word which contains the absent consonant sound **w** pronounced in combination with the vowel element **o-e**, other than the related word **once**.

4. ou   (rough, tough)

rough -   See *ruff*   (1.u - p.72)
tough -   See *tuff*   (1.u - p.74)

XI - The Long Diphthong Sound of OO

Alphabetic Representation	Sound-symbol Representation	Number of Homonyms
1. oo	boot, too	25
2. ew	brew, threw	13
3. u-e	lute, ruse	12
4. ou	roux, through	9
5. ue	blue, rue	9
6. ui	bruise, cruise	4
7. u	flu, gnu	4
8. o	do, two	3
9. oe	shoe	1
10. eu	rheum	1
11. ieu	lieu	1

Total - 82 Homonyms

Note: See Also IX (Long U Sound)

1. oo   (too, boot)

boos* - See *booze* (1.oo - p.75)
booze -   (Informal) *The old man likes to drink booze.*
   (alcoholic drinks) or *He is going out to booze with his friends.*
     Also: *boos* - plural form of *boo* - *I heard many boos coming from the crowd.* or a present tense form of *to boo* - *The fan boos his team.*
brood - *The parents watched over their brood in the nest.*
   or *Mother calls her children her brood.* or *Before*

75

the eggs will hatch, the parents have *to* ***brood*** (sit on the eggs). or *Why does the poet* ***brood*** (ponder moodily) *so often?*
    Also: ***brewed*** - past tense form of *to brew* - *Dad* ***brewed*** *a pot of coffee for us.*

choose - *Why did they* ***choose*** *you to be class president?*
    Also: ***chews*** - plural form of *chew* - *He gave me two* ***chews*** *of tobacco.* or a present tense form of *to chew* - *The old dog* ***chews*** *the bone noisily.*

coop - *The farmer kept his chickens in a* ***coop.*** or (Slang) *The two thieves flew the* ***coop*** (escaped). or *He tried to* ***coop*** *up his wife, but she didn't like it.*
    Also: ***coupe*** - *A* ***coupe*** *is a dessert of ice cream or fruit ices, garnished with nuts and whipped cream, served in a special dish.*

gloom - *We sensed a feeling if* ***gloom*** *in the house.* or *The sad news will* ***gloom*** *everyone.*
    Also: ***glume*** - *A* ***glume*** *is a chaffy basal bract on a spikelet of grass.*

loo - *Loo is a kind of card game.* (Shortened from *lanterloo.*)
    Also: ***lieu*** - *The worker was given food in* ***lieu*** *of* (in place of) *money.*

loon - *A* ***loon*** *can be either a diving sea bird or a simple minded person.*
    Also: ***lune*** - *A* ***lune*** *is a term used to describe a portion of a sphere.*

loop - *Jack made a* ***loop*** *in the rope when he tied the package.* or *The plane flew a* ***loop*** *over the airport.* or *He is going to* ***loop*** *the thread.* or *Did the plane* ***loop*** *above the field?*
    Also: ***loupe*** - *The jeweler put his* ***loupe*** *to his eye and examined the diamond.*

loot - *The robbers hid the* ***loot*** *in the cave.* or (Slang) *I can't lend you* ***loot*** (money) *because I'm broke.* or *The enemy forces will* ***loot*** *the captured town.*
    Also: ***lute*** - *The lutist played his* ***lute*** (a stringed instrument) *well.* or ***Lute*** *is a substance used to pack and seal joints and connections.*

mood - *The teacher was in a bad mood today.* or *The mood of the film was dark.*
    Also: *mooed* - past tense form of *to moo* - *The old cow mooed when she was mad.*
mooed* - See *mood* (1.oo - p.77)
pool - *We went for a swim in the new swimming pool.* or *My friends drive to work as part of a car pool.* or *I like to play pool with Tom.* or *We hired a new secretary from a pool of workers.* or *Let's pool our funds and buy a new car.*
    Also: *pul* - *A pul is a coin used in Afghanistan.*
rood - *A rood is a type of cross or crucifix.* or (British) *A rood is a measure of length.*
    Also: *rude* - *That boy was very rude* (uncouth) *to his teacher.* or *They crossed over a rude* (crude) *bridge.*
    Also: *rued* - past tense form of *to rue* - *Bob rued* (regretted) *the day he joined the club.*
room - *My room was large and sunny.* or *His desk uses too much room.* or *I went to room in a big hotel.*
    Also: *rheum* - *Rheum is a watery mucous which is discharged from the eyes or nose.*
root - *The root of a growing thing usually grows under the ground.* or *The root of a family includes ancestors.* or *A root is a term used in mathematics.* or *The plant will root quickly.* or *A pig likes to root in the ground with its snout.*
    Also: *route* [1] - *A route is a course or a way to travel from one place to another.* or *The dispatcher will route all its traffic away from the accident.*
    (See *route*[2] - XV- 1. ou -rout - p.91)
shoo - (Interjection) *Shoo! Go away!* or *We tried to shoo the pesky cat away.*
    Also: *shoe* - *My shoe doesn't fit well.* or *The blacksmith put a new shoe on the horse.* or *My brake shoe is worn down.* or *When will he come to shoe the horses?*
shoot - *The plant put out a new shoot.* or *The small raft went over the shoot* (rapid). or *The models got dressed for the film shoot.* or *Why did he shoot*

the animal? or The raft will **shoot** the rapids. or The man couldn't **shoot** the door bolt.
>Also: **chute** - The water flowed down the **chute**. or (Informal) My **chute** (parachute) wouldn't open.

soot [2] - The chimney sweep cleaned out the **soot** [2] from the walls of the chimney. (The most common pronunciation **soot**[1] would rhyme with foot)
>Also: **suit** - Dad bought a new **suit** for the party. or Which **suit** of cards in the deck do you like the best? or The man brought **suit** in court to regain his property. or This car is not going to **suit** your taste in colors. or It is two o'clock and time for the team to **suit** up.

stoop - The old man had a **stoop** as he walked. or Everyone was sitting on the **stoop** in front of the house. or Dad had to **stoop** over when he entered the room. or Why do you **stoop** to making such petty insults?
>Also: ***stupe*** [1] - A **stupe** is a hot medicated compress.

too - You can go to the game **too** (also). or The man is **too** short, **too** fat, **too** ugly, etc.
>Also: **to** - as part of the infinitive form: **to** go, **to** drive, **to** think, **to** slide, **to** run, etc. or (Preposition) I went **to** the store, **to** the game, **to** a movie, **to** school, etc.
>Also: **two** - I see **two** cats, **two** cars, **two** people, **two** stars, **two** books, etc.

tool - A **tool** is an instrument operated by hand, such as a hammer or a hoe. or A **tool**, such as a lathe, is also a type of **tool**. or Didn't he know he was simply a **tool** (dupe) in their evil plans? or He will **tool** (work or form) the finished products at his workbench.
>Also: ***tulle*** - **Tulle** is a fine starched net of silk or rayon used for veils or gowns.

toon - **Toon** is the name of a tall tree found in Australia or tropical Asia.
>Also: ***tune*** [1] - The band played a great old **tune**. or The president isn't in **tune** with the times. or The

   man came to tune our old piano. (In **tune**² the sound of the vowel is that heard in *cue* or *muse.*)
troop - *A **troop** of soldiers were camped by the river.* or *The boy scouts are going to **troop** over the hill and have a meal.*
  Also: **troupe** - *The **troupe** of touring actors put on a play.* or *The theater company will **troupe** over the countryside.*
zoo - *The wild animals in the **zoo** were very upset.*
  Also: **xu** - *The **xu** is a coin used in North Vietnam.*
* A root with an inflection

2. **ew** (brew, threw)

blew - irregular past tense form of *to blow* - *When the wind **blew**, the sailboat moved swiftly.*
  Also: **blue** - ***Blue** is a color, a pigment, or a dye.* or *Policemen are sometimes called the men in **blue**.* or *During the Civil War, a soldier in the Union army was sometimes referred to as a **blue**.* or (Theater) *Risque humor is often referred to as **blue**.* or *She is going to **blue*** (add bluing) *the dress.* or *Tom was feeling very **blue**.*
brewed* - See **brood** (1.oo - p.75)
chews* - See **choose** (1.oo - p.76)
clew - *A ball or yarn is called a **clew**. In Greek Mythology, it was the thread used by Theseus to guide him through the labyrinth of Minos on Crete.* or *A **clew** is one of the corners on a square sail.* or *I had to **clew** the thread into a ball.*
  Also: **clue** - *The police were looking for a **clue**.* or *I will **clue** you when I want you to answer.* (Variant spelling **clew**)
crewed* - See **crude** (3.u-e - p.82)
crews* - See **cruise** (6.ui - p.82)
dew - *The **dew** collected on the morning grass.* or *The damp air will **dew** the ground.*
  (**dew**² rhymeswith **cue** or **few**.)

Also: *due* - *They paid the old man his **due**.* or *When is the payment **due**?* or *We set our course for **due** east.*
(*due*² rhymes with *cue* or *few*.)
Also: *do* - *When will you **do** your work?* or *This place will **do** very well.*

flew - irregular past tense form of *to fly* - *The bird **flew** up to its vest.*
Also: *flue* - *A **flue** is a pipe, or tube, through which air, gas, steam, or smoke may pass.* or *Flue may also be the detritus of textile fabrics or fur, or it may be a kind of fishing net.*
Also: *flu* - *The word **flu** is a shortened version of a condition called influenza.*

knew - irregular past tense form of *to know* - *He got to the station before ten, because he **knew** the train would be early.*
Also: *new* - *Dad bought the car **new**.* or *The astronomer found a **new** star.* or *Don't expect too much yet because I'm **new** at this job.*
Also: *gnu* - *The **gnu** is a type of African antelope.*

new - See *knew* (2.ew - p.80)

slew - (Informal) *Bill has a whole **slew** of friends.* or irregular past tense form of *to slay* - *Cain **slew** Abel in the garden.* (Variant spelling *slue*.)
Also: *slue* - *The truck went into a **slue*** (a twisting slide). or *The truck is going to **slue** if it doesn't slow down.* (Variant spelling *slew*)
Also: *slough*¹ - *The wagon became stuck in a **slough**.* or *The poor family lived in a **slough*** (a backwater or bayou).
(*slough*² rhymes with *cow* or *brow*.)

threw - irregular past tense form of *to throw* - *He **threw** the ball to the base late.*
Also: *through* - *The ball went crashing **through** the window.* or *We live on a busy **through** street.*

yew - *The **yew** is a type of evergreen tree or shrub.*
Also: *you* - (Pronoun) *You are not my friend.* or *Did Tom hit **you**?*

* A root with an inflection

3. ue   (blue, rue)

blue -   See *blew*   (2.ew - p.79)
clue -   See *clew*   (2.ew - p.79)
due -   See *dew*   (2.ew - p.79)
flue -   See *flew*   (2.ew - p.80)
rue -   A *rue* is an aromatic Eurasian plant. or *I rue* (regret) the day I met him.
         Also: *roux* - A *roux* is a mixture of flour and butter which is browned together and used as a thickener in cooking.
rued* - See *rood*   (1.oo - p.77)
rues* - See *ruse*   (3.u-e - p.82)
slue -   See *slew*   (2.ew - p.80)
sue -   The lawyer advised me *to sue* the tenant for damage to my home. or The small country wanted *to sue* (appeal) for an end to the war.
         Also: *Sioux* - *Sioux* is the name applied to several North American peoples who once lived around the Great Plains.
* A root with an inflection

4. ou   (roux, through)

coupe -   See *coop*   (1.oo - p.76)
loupe -   See *loop*   (1.oo - p.76)
route¹ -   See *root*   (1.oo - p.77)
roux -   See *rue*   (5.ue - p.81)
rouxs* -   See *ruse*   (3.u-e - p.82)
slough¹ - See *slew*   (2.ew - p.80)
troupe -   See *troop*   (1.oo - p.79)
through - See *threw*   (2.ew - p.80)
you -   See *yew*   (2.ew - p.80)
* A root with an inflection

5. u-e   (lute, ruse)

brute - *That animal is a terrible looking brute.* <u>or</u> *He used brute strength to lift it up.*
    Also: *bruit* - *Bruit is a term used in medicine to describe a certain type of abnormal sound.* <u>or</u> *Don't bruit it about, but I won the lottery.*
chute - See *shoot*   (1.oo - p.77)
crude - *Jack is a very crude person.* <u>or</u> *The stove uses crude oil.*
    Also: *crewed* - past tense form of *to crew* - *Tom and Peggy crewed for me in the big yacht race.*
cruse - See *cruise*   (6.ui - p.82)
glume - See *gloom*   (1.oo - p.76)
lune - See *loon*   (1.oo - p.76)
lute - See *loot*   (1.oo - p.76)
rude - See *rood*   (1.oo - p.77)
ruse - *He tricked his friend with a clever ruse.*
    Also: *rues* - a present tense form of *to rue* - *Jack rues the day you came back*
    Also: plural form of *roux* - *The cook made two rouxs.*
stupe - See *stoop*   (1.oo - p.78)
tulle - See *tool*   (1.oo - p.78)
tune - See *toon*   (1.oo - p.78)

6. ui   (bruise, cruise)

bruise - *When I fell down, I got a bruise on my knee.* <u>or</u> *Such an insult will bruise his feelings.*
    Also: *brews* - plural form of *brew* - *There are two different brews of coffee I enjoy most.* <u>or</u> a present tense form of *to brew* - *Mother brews delicious tea.*
bruit - See *brute*   (3.u-e - p.82)
cruise - *We took a cruise along the coast last summer.* <u>or</u> *Let's cruise around the lake today.*
    Also: *cruse* - *A cruse is a small jar or pot for holding water, oil, or wine.*

Also: *crews* - plural form of *crew* - *The ships changed their crews for every voyage.*

suit - See *soot* ²   (1.oo - p.78)

7. u   (flu, gnu)

flu -	See *flew*	(2.ew - p.80)
gnu -	See *knew*	(2.ew - p.80)
pul -	See *pool*	(1.oo - p.77)
xu -	See *zoo*	(1.oo - p.79)

8. o   (do, two)

do -	See *dew*	(2.ew - p.83)
to -	See *too*	(1.oo) - p.78)
two -	See *too*	(1.oo - p.78)

9. oe   (shoe)

shoe - See *shoo*   (1.oo - p.77)

10. eu   (rheum)

rheum - See *room*   (1.oo - p.77)

11. ieu   (lieu)

lieu - See *loo*   (1.oo - p.76)

XII - The Short Diphthong Sound of OO

Alphabetic Representation	Sound-symbol Representation	Number of Homonyms
1. oo	book, foot	1
2. ou	would	1

Total - 2 Homonyms

1. **oo** (book, foot)

wood - *Dad bought a pile of **wood** for the fire.* <u>or</u> *The class went for a walk in the **wood**.* <u>or</u> *The child's toys were made of **wood**.* <u>or</u> *He tried to **wood** (reforest) the land with new trees.*
    Also: *would* - past tense form of *will* - *I **would** go, but I have no ticket.* <u>or</u> ***Would** you take me home now?*

2. **ou** (would)

would - See *wood*   (1.**oo** - p.84)

XIII - The Diphthong Sound of AU

Alphabetic Representation	Sound-symbol Representation	Number of Homonyms
1. au	haul, taught	11
2. a	all, bald	8
3. aw	law, dawn	7
4. ou	ought	1

Total - 27 Homonyms

1. au   (haul, taught)

aught - *Aught is a cipher meaning zero.* or *For aught (all) we know, he may never have left.* (Alternate spelling **ought**)
   Also: **ought** - normally used as an auxiliary verb followed by an infinitive with *to - He ought to work harder.* or *The train ought to arrive on time today.*
caul - *The caul is a membrane that covers the developing infant in its mother's womb.*
   Also: **call** - *The animal heard the call of the wild.* or *I call that a fair deal.* or *I gave him a call on the phone last night.* or *She is going to call home today.*
caulk - *A boatmaker will caulk a boat to seal cracks, and a plumber will caulk pipes or fittings to make them airtight or watertight.*
   Also: **calk** - *A calk is a pointed extension on the heel or toe of a horseshoe to prevent slipping.* or *The woman had a calk on the sole of her shoes to stop her from slipping.* or *We call a blacksmith or a shoemaker to calk different types of shoes.*
cause - *The soldier died for a glorious cause.* or *What was the cause of the disturbance?* or *He tried to cause an argument.*
   Also: **caws** - plural form of *caw* - *I could hear the caws of the crows in the tree.* or present tense

form of *to caw* - *The crow sits in the tree and caws.*
clause - *What is the main clause in the sentence?* or *There was a clause in the contract I didn't like.*
  Also: **claws** - plural form of *claw* - *The cat's claws were sharp.* or present tense form of *to claw* - *The bear claws at his keeper.*
haul - *The thieves made quite a haul from the bank.* or *It's a long haul from my house to yours.* or *The man came to haul the rubbish away.*
  Also: **hall** - *The class had to wait in the hall.* or *The group entered the hall.*
maul - *The worker hit the spike with a heavy maul* (hammer). or *Why did the bear try to maul the hunter?* (Variant spelling **mall**.)
  Also: **mall** - *A wide mall divided the highway.* or *The children went to shop at the mall.*
Paul -   See **pawl**   (2.aw - p.87)
pause - *There was a slight pause and then the music started again.* or *The speaker had to pause before he could go on.*
  Also: **paws** - plural form of *paw* - *The dog put his paws on top of the sleeping child.* or present tense form of *to paw* - *The animal paws the meat then eats it.*
taught - See **taut**   (1.au - p.86)
taut - *The rope was so taut* (tight), *it broke.*
   Also: **taught** - irregular past tense form of *to teach* - *The child was taught never to tell a lie.*

2. a   all, bald

all -   See **awl**   (3.aw - p.87)
bald - *The old man's head was completely bald.*
   Also: **bawled** - past tense form of *to bawl* - *The child bawled when he dropped his ice cream.*
ball -   See **bawl**   (3.aw - p.87)
call -   See **caul**   (1.au - p.85)

calk - See *caulk*   (1.au - p.85)
hall - See *haul*   (1.au - p.86)
mall - See *maul*   (1.au - p.86)
pall - See *pawl*   (3.aw - p.87)

3. aw   law, dawn

awl - *The shoemaker punched holes in the leather with an awl.*
  Also: *all* - *We all went to the game.* or *Can I have all of the food that is left?*
bawl - *The child fell down and started to bawl* (cry out loudly). or *Why did the teacher want to bawl* (scold loudly) *you out?*
  Also: *ball* - *The children had a red beach ball.* or *The princess went to the ball.* or *The rocket blasted off in a ball of fire.* or *That worker is on the ball.*
bawled* - See *bald*   (2.a - p.87)
caws* - See *cause*   (1.au - p.85)
claws* - See *clause*   (1.au - p.86)
pawl - *A pawl is a type of hinged or pivoted device.*
  Also: *pall* - *They covered the coffin with a black pall.* or *A coffin, on its way to a tomb, is called a pall.* or *A heavy black pall of black smoke hung over the city.* or *Jack tends to pall* (become boring or wearisome) *when one is near him too long.*
  Also: *Paul* - a masculine given name.
paws* - See *pause*   (1.au - p.86)
* A root with an inflection

4. ou   ought

ought - See *aught*   (1.au - p.85)

XIV - The Diphthong Sound of OI

Alphabetic Representation	Sound-symbol Representation	Number of Homonyms
1. oi	boil, oil	3
2. oy	boy, toy	1
3. uoy	buoy	1

Total - 5 Homonyms

1. oi   boil, oil

coin - *Do you have the correct* **coin** *for this purchase?* or *In architecture, a* **coin** *is a cornerstone or a corner.* or *The men at the mint are going to* **coin** *silver dollars today.*
   Also: **quoin** - *A* **quoin** *is a stone used to form an angle of a wall, or masonry, or a cornerstone.* or *In printing, a* **quoin** *is a wedge-shaped block used to lock type in place.* or *The builder had to* **quoin** (secure or support) *the building to make it secure.*
pois* - See *poise*   (1.oi - p.88)
poise - *The speaker demonstrated a great deal of* **poise**. or **Poise** *is a measure of dynamic viscosity.* or *Why did he* **poise** (balance) *himself at the edge of the cliff?*
   Also: **pois** - plural form of *poi* - *Hawaiians eat several types of food called* **pois**.
quoin - See *coin*   (1.oi - p.88)
roil - *Try not to* **roil** (disturb, vex, or cloud) *the water.*
   Also: **royal** - a word used as a noun or an adjective.
   Note: Although this word is not a homonym of *roil,* rather it is an example of a "sound misperception," one which causes a serious problem for poor spellers. It appears here only to help those who hear these two words as being the same, whatever the initial cause of such confusion may be. It usually is misheard in sentences such as: *The* **royal** *is a*

sail which is set on the royal mast. or *The king and queen entered the **royal** palace.* It is properly pronounced in two syllables, as *roy al,* and **not** as *roil.*
* A root with an inflection

2. **oy**   (boy, toy)

boy - *The small **boy** was playing on the swings.* or (Interjection) ***Boy!** Was I surprised to see you.*
  Also: ***buoy**²* - *We tied the boat to the **buoy** because we were lost.* or *The sailor is going to **buoy*** (mark with buoys)*the channel.* or *The message will **buoy*** (raise or uplift)*his spirits.*
  (**Note:** Although the most common pronunciation of *buoy* is as *boo ee,* the pronunciation presented here is very commonly used and acceptable.)

3.**uoy**   (buoy)

buoy ² - See *boy*   (2.**oy** - p.89)

XV - The Diphthong Sound of OU

Alphabetic Representation	Sound-symbol Representation	Number of Homonyms
1. ou	loud, out	9
2. ow	cow, sow	4

Total - 13 Homonyms

1. **ou** (loud, out)

bough - *A bough is a large tree branch.*
>Also: **bow** - *The front of a ship, or boat, is called the bow.* or *The actor took another bow.* or *He asked me to bow before I left the king's room.*

flour - *The baker uses a lot of flour to make bread.* or *He had to flour the board before rolling the dough.*
>Also: **flower** - a word used as a noun or verb.
>Note: Although this word is not a homonym of *flour,* it is an example of a "sound misperception," one which causes a serious problem for poor spellers. It appears here only to help those who hear these two words as being the same, whatever the initial cause of such confusion may be. It usually is misheard in sentences such as, *The florist put a flower in the vase.* or *The plant began to flower too early.* It is properly pronounced as though it were spelled as *flow er,* and **not** as *flour.*

foul - *Something foul is blocking the path.* or *The hitter hit a fly ball, but the umpire said it was foul.* or *I hope I don't foul* (commit a breach of the rules) *him again.* or *The smoke will foul the air roday.* or *Why did the boxer try to foul his opponent?*
>Also: **fowl** - *A fowl is a type of bird used for either food or game.* or *The men are going to fowl* (hunt) *for game birds.*

hour -   See *our*   (1.**ou** - p.91)

our - possessive form of the pronoun *us* - *These are our children.* or *We achieved all of our goals.*
  Also: *hour* - (pronounced as **our**) *I'll meet you in one hour.* or *There are sixty minutes in one hour.*
rouse - *The bugle call served as a rouse for the troops.* or *Dad couldn't rouse me from my deep sleep.*
  Also: *rows* ² - plural form of *row* - *The family had terrible rows* (quarrels or brawls) *almost every day.* or *The man rows with his wife constantly.*
rout - *The enemy retreat was a complete rout.* or *The general hoped to rout the enemy.* or *The pig uses its snout to rout through the garbage.*
  Also: *route* ² - *We followed the same route as the pioneers.* or *The dispatcher tried to route the bus away from the storm.*
  (See also XI - 1. oo - root - p.77)
route ² - See *rout*   (1.ou - p.91)
sough ² - *I could hear the wind sough through the trees.*
  (**Sough**¹ rhymes with **snuff**.)
  Also: *sow* - *A sow is an adult female hog.* or *A mass of moten metal in solidified form is called a sow.*

2. o w   (c o w, s o w)

*brows** - See *browse*   (2.ow - p.91)
browse - *Mother likes to browse in all the shops for bargains.* or *The deer will browse on the leaves.*
  Also: *brows* - plural form of *brow* - *The audience raised their brows at the play.*
*flower** - See *flour*   (1.ou - p.90)
rows ² * - See *rouse*   (1.ou - p.91)
sow -   See *sough* ²   (1.ou - p.91)
* A root with an inflection

XVI - The r-Controlled Sound of AR

Alphabetic Representation	Sound-symbol Representation	Number of Homonyms
1. ar	art, far, hard	16
2. ear	heart	1

Total - 17 Homonyms

1. ar   (art, far, hard)

arc - *Arc is a word used for anything shaped like a bow, curve, or arch.* or *The term* arc *is used with a specific meaning in the fields of mathematics, geometry, and electricity.* or *The electrical charge is going to arc now.*
   Also: ark - *Noah built an* ark. or *The chest containing the stone tablets with the ten commandments on them, and carried by the Hebrews during their wanderings in the desert, was referred to as "the* ark *of the covenant."*
ark -   See *arc*   (1.ar - p.92)
bard - *A* bard *is a name given to a poet, especially one who is well known.* or *Armor used to protect or tournament a horse was referred to as* bard. or *The knight went to* bard (equip with bards)*his horse.*
   Also: past tense form of *to bar* - *The boxer was* barred *from ever fighting there again.*
bark - *The* bark *of the tree had been peeled away.* or *Did you hear a dog's* bark? or *The lumberjack was sent to* bark (remove the bark from)*the tall tree.* or *The dog is going to* bark *all night.*
   Also: barque - *A* barque *was a sailing ship having from three to five masts.* (Also bark)
barred* - See *bard*   (1.ar - p.92)
barque - See *bark*   (1.ar - p.92)
chard - *Chard is a variety of beet having large leaves.*
   Also: charred - past tense form of *to char* - *The fire* charred (scorched)*the fine old wood surface.*
charred* - See *chard*   (1.ar - p.92)

czar - Czar was the name of the former emperors of Russia. or A tyrant or autocrat is sometimes called a czar. (Informal) A person in authority is sometimes referred to as a czar, as in "labor czar." (zar)
    Also: **tsar** - a variant spelling for **czar** (zar).
hart - A hart is a male deer, especially a male red deer of more than five years of age.
    Also: **heart** - The man died when his heart stopped pumping. or Everyone says that fighter has the heart of a lion. or He made his speech with a heavy heart. or Our store is in the heart of the business district.
marc - Marc is the pulpy residue left after the juice has been squeezed from grapes, apples, or other fruits. or The farmer made marc from the apple residue.
    Also: **mark** - The paint left a mark on the old wall. or The teacher gave me a good mark. or The illiterate man placed his mark on the contract. or Who is going to mark all of these test papers? or The pirate wanted to mark the spot where he buried the treasure.
mark - See marc   (1.ar - p.93)
par - Jack wasn't feeling up to par. or Par is the face value of a monetary unit in terms of other currencies with which it is compared. or Par is the number of stokes considered necessary to go from the tee to the hole.
    Also: **parr** - A young salmon living in fresh water during the first two years of its life is called a parr.
pard - (Archaic) A leopard was once called a pard.
    Also: **parred** - (Slang) past tense form of to par - The golfer parred the ninth hole easily.
parr - See par   (1.ar - p.93)
parred * - See pard   (1.ar - p.93)
tsar - See czar   (1.ar - p.93)
* A root with an inflection

2. ear heart

heart - See hart   (1.ar - p.93)

XVIIA - The r-Controlled Sounds of OR

Alphabetic Representation	Sound-symbol Representation	Number of Homonyms
1. or	or, fort	23
2. oar	boar, hoarse	8
3. ore	core, sore	8
4. our	four, mourn	6
5. ar	quart, quartz	4
6. oor	door	1
7. orr	torr	1

Total - 51 Homonyms

1. or   (or, fort)

bored* - See **board**   (2.oa - p.95)
chord - She played a **chord** on the piano. or That speech struck a resonant **chord**. or I will **chord** the piece for the recording.
    Also: **cord** - Can I use this **cord** to tie the package? or His spinal **cord** was badly damaged. or I need a **cord** of wood for the fireplace. or Please **cord** (tie) the papers for me.
    Also: **cored** - past tense form of to core - My father **cored** the apple for me.
cord -   See **chord** -   (1.or - p.94)
corps -   See **core**   (3.ore - p.97)
corse -   See **coarse**   (2.oar - p.96)
dor -   A **dor** is a type of droning insect, as the **dor**beetle.
    Also: **door** - He opened the **door** and entered the room. or I live just one **door** away from you.
for -   See **fore**   (3.ore - p.97)
fort - When the **fort** was attacked, the soldiers barred the doors.
    Also: **forte** - His fine acting ability was his **forte** (strong point). or The strong part of a sword blade is called the **forte**.

94

forte - See *fort*   (1.or - p.94)
forth - We came *forth* from the darkness into the light.
    Also: *fourth* - He inherited a *fourth* of his father's
    fortune. or The little girl celebrated her *fourth*
    birthday.
horde -   See *hoard*   (2.oar - p.96)
horse -   See *hoarse*   (2.oar - p.96)
kor -   See *core*   (3.o-e - p.97)
morn -   See *mourn*   (4.our - p.98)
or -   See *oar*   (2.oar - p.97)
tor -   A *tor* is a high hill, or a pile of rocks atop a hill.
    Also: *tore* - *Tore* is also a term used in geometry or
    architecture. or irregular past tense form of *to tear*
    - The boy *tore* his pants on a nail.
    Also: *torr* - A *torr* is a unit of atmospheric pressure
torr -   See *tor*   (1.or - p.95)
sord - A flight of mallards (wild ducks) is called a *sord*.
    Also: *sword* - Why did the man duel with a *sword*?
sword -   See *sord*   (1.or - p.95)
wort [2] - See *wart*   (5.ar - p.98)
* A root with an inflection

2. oar   (boar, horse)

boar - A *boar* is either an uncastrated male pig, or a wild
    pig.
    Also: *bore* - The men made a *bore*, or hole, through
    the stone wall. or The *bore* is the caliber of a gun.
    or Johnny is such a *bore* (a dull person). or
    There is a type of dangerous wave which is called a
    bore. or The driller has *to bore* the hole by
    noon. or Why does he *bore* (be tedious) everyone
    with his stories?
board - The carpenter nailed the *board* over the window.
    or Dad is a member of the *board*. or She
    worked at the hotel for room and *board*. or The
    men went *to board* up the old building. or Mary
    wants *to board* a pet while she's away.

Also: **bored** - past tense form of *to bore* - *He bored a hole in the wall.* or *Jack bored his friend with a long tale.*

coarse - *Why is that man so coarse* (lacking refinement)? or *He filled the bag with coarse sand.*

Also: **course** - *We followed the swift course of the river.* or *His life seems to be taking a different course now.* or *The navigator plotted the new course the plane would fly.* or *We played two rounds of golf on the new course.* or *Of course you can come to my party.* or *The blood began to course through his veins once again.* or *Where are the hunters going to course* (hunt) *for the game animals?* or *Santa's reindeer will course through the sky.*

Also: **corse** - (Archaic) *A corpse and a corse were once words with the same meaning.*

hoar - *The meaning of the noun hoar is whiteness; as an adjective it appears as hoary.*

Also: **whore** - *A whore is a prostitute.* or *The verb to whore means to act as a prostitute.*

hoard - *The miser hid a hoard under the floor.* or *It is wrong to hoard food* (accumulate selfishly) *during wartime.*

Also: **horde** - *A horde is a swarm, or throng, of people, animals, or insects.* or *The Mongols came in a horde.* or *The insects began to horde.*

Also: **whored** - past tense form of *to whore* - *The prostitute whored for money.*

hoarse - *What made his voice sound hoarse as he spoke?* or *He voice had a hoarse* (throaty) *quality.*

Also: **horse** - *The little girl rode her horse around the track.* or *An adult male horse is referred to as a horse.* or *The carpenter placed some boards on a horse* (a wooden support frame with four legs). or *The man is going to horse* (provide with a horse) *his mistress.* or *The teacher told his students not to horse* (engage in horseplay) *around.*

oar - The rower put his *oar* into the water. or Jack was an *oar* (rower) on the team. or It took an hour to *oar* across the river.
    Also: *ore* - *Ore* is a mineral which has a valuable component, usually metal, such as iron ore.
    Also: *or* - (Conjunction) You can go *or* stay. or Either you do what I say, *or* you must leave.
soar - The man went for a *soar.* or The glider will *soar* through the clear blue sky.
    Also: *sore* - Will the doctor take care of the *sore* on my arm? or My *sore* arm kept me from playing.

3. ore   (core, sore)

bore - See *boar*   (2.oar - p.95)
core - The apple *core* is the part which contains the seeds. or The heart serves as the *core* of the human being. or The nuclear reactor needed a new *core*. or Mom had to *core* the apples.
    Also: *kor* - A *kor* was an ancient Hebrew unit of dry or liquid measure; it was also called a "homer".
    Also: *corps* - The boy played in the drum *corps*. or A *corps* is a separate branch of the military. (plural form also *corps*)
cored* - See *chord*   (1.or - p.94)
fore - The bow, or the front part of a ship, is also called the *fore*. or (Interjection) *Fore!* A warning used in golf to signal that a ball has been stroked nearby.
    Also: *four* - May I have *four* (4) candies?
    Also: *for* - (Preposition) I went to the store *for* my friend. or *For* my country, I would give my life.
gored* - See *gourd*   (4.ou - p.98)
ore -   See *oar*   (2.oar - p.97)
sore -   See *soar*   (2.oar - p.97)
tore -   See *tor*   (1.or - p.95)
whore - See *hoar*   (2.oar - p.96)
wore -   See *war*   (5.ar - p.98)

4. our   (four, mourn)

course - See *coarse* (2.oar - p.96)
four - See *fore* (3.ore - p.97)
fourth - See *forth* (1.or - p.95)
gourd - The *gourd* is an unusually shaped fruit that grows on a vine. or The shell of a *gourd* is sometimes used as a drinking vessel.
    Also: *gourde* - The *gourde* is the basic monetary unit of Haiti.
    Also: *gored* - past tense form of *to gore* - The man was *gored* by the raging bull.
gourde - See *gourd* (4.our - p.98)
mourn - Will the family members *mourn* their father?
    Also: *morn* - (Poetic) The sun rose on the wings of *morn* (morning).

5. ar   (quart, quartz)

quarts* - See *quartz* (5.ar - p.98)
quartz - *Quartz* is a kind of hard, crystalline, vitreous mineral found in sandstone.
    Also: *quarts* - May I have two *quarts* of milk? or If, while playing cards, two of the players had hands with two *quarts* in them, they would both have sequences of four playing cards in one suit.
war - The two countries are at *war*. or The king made *war* on his neighbors.
    Also: *wore* - irregular past tense form of *to wear* - She *wore* the crown proudly.
wart - He had a large *wart* (abnormal growth) on his hand.
    Also: *wort* [2] - The *wort* is a plant, like the milkwort. or *Wort* is a liquid with malt added to make beer. (*wort*[1] rhymes with **hurt**.)

* A root with an inflection

6. oor   (door)

door - See *dor* (1.or - p.94)

7. orr   (torr)

torr - See *tor* (1.or - p.95)

XVIIB The r-Controlled Sound of OR (world)

Alphabetic Representation	Sound-symbol Representation	Number of Homonyms
1. or	word, world	4

Total - 4 Homonyms

1. or   (word, world)

whorl - A **whorl** is a small flywheel that regulates the speed of a spinning wheel. or A **whorl** can also be a coil, curl, or a convolution. or **Whorl** is also a term used in the fields of botany, zoology, and architecture. (**wh** properly pronounced as *hw*)
  Also: **whirl** - We gave the top a good **whirl**. or He told me to give life a **whirl**. or My mind was in a **whirl**. or The top began to **whirl** wildly. (**wh** properly pronounced as *hw*) See XIX (ir - 104))
word - A **word** is a group of sounds, or alphabetic letters, which in totality carry a meaning for either a producer of receiver of the intended message. or Did you get the **word** from headquarters yet? or He had to **word** his message carefully.
  Also: **whirred** - past tense form of *to whir* - The arrow **whirred** through the air. (**wh** properly pronounced as *hw*) See XIX (ir - p.104)
world - The **world** is usually defined as the earth and its people. or Each time I read a book, I enter the **world** of the imagination. or He travels in the **world** of the arts. or He said he felt like he was on top of the **world**.
  Also: **whirled** - past tense form of *to whirl* - Tom **whirled** the disk at me. (**wh** properly pronounced as *hw*) See XIX (ir - p.104)
worst - See **wurst** XX (ur - p.105)

XVIII - The r-Controlled Sound of ER

Alphabetic Representation	Sound-symbol Representation	Number of Homonyms
1. er	herd, tern	10
2. ear	earn, pearl	3
3. ere	were	2
4. ier	tierce	1

Total - 16 Homonyms

1. er   (herd, tern)

berth - *The liner was moved into its waiting berth.* or *Who slept in the upper berth on the train trip?* or *The ship's mate was looking for a berth on the ship.* or *Are you going to berth your yacht here?*
Also: **birth** - *The father was present at the birth of his daughter.* or *The Bill of Rights was formulated during the birth of a new nation.* or *Jodie wants to birth* (bear) *a child at home.* See **XIX** (ir - p.100)

herd - *The herd of cows grazed in the pasture.* or *He fired a shot into the herd of elephants.* or *Where is the cowboy going to herd all of these steers?*
Also: **heard** - irregular past tense form of *to hear* - *Last night I heard a wild animal cry in the night.*

hertz - *A hertz is a unit of frequency.*
Also: **hurts** - plural form of *hurt* - *I was the victim of hurts at Tom's hands.* See **XX** (ur - p.105)

per - *The cost of the gas was twenty cents per* (for each) *gallon.* or *He was paid on a per diem* (for each day) *basis.*
Also: **purr** - *The purr of a cat indicates contentment.* or *The cat will purr when I rub her nose.* See **XX** (ur - p.105)

serf - *A serf was from the feudal class, the lowest class of society in medieval Europe. It is also a term applied now to any person in servitude.*

Also: **surf** - *Offshore waters, or waves, are called* **surf.** or *Are you going to* **surf** *on your new surf board?* See **XX** (**ur** - p.105)
serge - *My first suit was blue and made of* **serge.**
Also: **surge** - *The huge wave can* **surge** *and swamp the boat.* or *A* **surge** *of electricty caused the power station to shut down.* or *The ocean will* **surge** *and wash over everything.* See **XX** (**ur** - p.105)
tern - *A* **tern** *is a type of sea bird which resembles a gull.* or *A* **tern** *is a term used to designate groups of three (3), or a three-masted schooner.*
Also: **turn** - *Will you meet us at the* **turn** *in the road?* or *Has the sick dog taken a* **turn** *for the worse?* or *The gardener tries to* **turn** *the soil often.* or *The merchant is only trying to* **turn** *a small profit.* See **XX** (**ur** - p.105)
terce - See **tierce** (4.**ier** - p.102)
terse - *The doctor gave his patient a very* **terse** (exact) *answer.*
Also: **tierce** - **Tierce** *is the third of the seven canonical hours; it is also the name given to the time set aside for prayer at this hour.* or *In card games,* **tierce** *means a sequence of three cards of the same suit.* or **Tierce** *is also a term used in fencing and music.* (Variant spelling - **terce**)
twerp - (Slang) *A* **twerp** *is a small, despicable person.*
(Variant spelling **twirp** - See **XIX** (**ir** - p.104)
* A root with an inflection

2. **ear** (earn, pearl)

earn - *Do you* **earn** *much money as a cook?*
Also: **urn** - *Mother placed fresh flowers in the old* **urn.** or *May I draw a fresh cup of tea for you from the* **urn?** or *An* **urn** *is a part of a moss capsule.* See **XX** (**ur** - p.105)
heard - See **herd** (1.**er** - p.100)
pearl - *The lucky child found a black* **pearl** *in her oyster.*
Also: **purl** - *A* **purl** *is a type of knitting stitch.*

(Variant spelling **pearl**) or *I am going to purl so I can finish the knitting.* or *I heard the purl* (rippling sound) *of the stream.* See **XX** (**ur** - p.105)

3. **ere** (were)

cere - See *sir* (**XIX** (1.ir - p.103)
were - as the complement of *was*, the singular and plural past tense forms of *to be* - *You **were** on time, but I **was** late.* or an auxiliary verb to complement a main verb - *We **were** running to catch the train.*
  Also: ***whir*** - *I like to hear the **whir** of a spinning top.* or *The top will **whir** as it moves.* **wh** properly pronounced as *hw*. See **whale I** (a-e - p.7) See **XIX** (**ir** - p.104)

4. **ier** (tierce)

tierce - See *terse* (1.er - p.101)

XIX - The r-Controlled Sound of IR

Alphabetic Representation	Sound-symbol Representation	Number of Homonyms
1. ir	birth, sir	10

Total - 10 Homonyms

1. ir (birth, sir)

bird - *The soaring bird flew gracefully through the sky.*
    Also: **burred** - past tense form of *to burr* - *He burred the edges of the can.* See **XX** (**ur** - p.104)
birl - *The noise sounded like a birl* (hum). or *The top began to birl.* or *He tried to birl* (spin) *the floating log.*
    Also: *The yarn had a burl* (knot) *in it.* or *The tree had a burl on it.* or *My job was to burl* (remove burls) *the finished cloth.* See **XX** (**ur** - p.104)
birr - *A birr is a whirring sound.*
    Also: **burr** - *The metalsmith removed the burr* (rough edge) *from the metal piece.* or *A burr is a washer that fits on a rivet.* or *The scotchman pronounces the letter "r" with a burr.* or *He will burr the metal edge.* or *Jock tends to burr his r's.* See **XX** (**ur** - p.104)
    Also: **bur** - *The bur* (rough prickly husk) *stuck to my clothing.* or *He has a personality like a bur* (something or someone that adheres persistently. (Variant spelling **burr**) See **XX** (**ur** - p.104)
birth - **berth** See **XVIII** (**er** - p.100)
fir - *A fir is a type of evergreen tree.*
    Also: **fur** - *An animal's hair covering is called its fur.* or *The craftsman is going to fur the garment.* or *Lining a wall or a door with strips of metal or wood is to fur it.* See **XX** (**ur** - p.104)

sir - The word *sir* is a respectful form of address used instead of a name, as "Thank you *sir*. or *Sir* is a title of honor used before the full name of baronets and knights.
    Also: *cere* - The mortician will *cere* (wrap)*the corpse in cerecloth*. See XVIII (3.ere - p.102)

twirp -   See *twerp* XVIII (1.er - p.101)
whir -   See *were* XVIII (3.ere - p.102)
whirl -   See *whorl* XVIIB (1.or - p.99)
whirled* -   See *world* XVIIB (1.or - p.99)
whirred* -   See *word* XVIIB (1.or - p.99)
* A root with an inflection

XX - The r-Controlled Sound of UR

Alphabetic Representation	Sound-symbol Representation	Number of Homonyms
1. ur	fur, hurt	15

Total - 15 Homonyms

1. ur   (fur, hurt)

bur - See *birr*   XIX (ir - p.103)
burg - A *burg* is a fortified town. or (Informal) A town or city is sometimes referred to as a *burg*.
  Also: *burgh* - A *burgh* is a chartered town or borough in Scotland.
burgh - See *burg*   (1.ur - p.104)
burl - See *birl*   XIX (ir - p.103)
burred* - See *bird*   XIX (ir - p.103)
curt - The girl gave the teacher a *curt* (rude or terse) answer to the question.
  Also: *Kurt* (a given name) fell off his horse.
  (Variant spelling - *Curt*)
fur - See *fir*   XIX (ir - p.103)
furs* - See *furze*   (1.ur - p.104)
furze - *Furze* is a spiny shrub, such as gorse.
  Also: *furs* - plural form of *fur* - The woman owned many fine *furs*.
hurts* - See *hertz*   XVIII (er - p.100)
purl - See *pearl*   XVIII (ear - p.102)
purr - See *per*   XVIII (er - p.101)
surf - See *serf*   XVIII (er - p.101)
surge - See *serge*   XVIII (er - p.101)
turn - See *tern*   XVIII (er - p.101)
urn - See *earn*   XVIII (er - p.102)
wurst - *Wurst* is a kind of sausage.
  Also: *worst* - superlative form of *bad* - That was the *worst* show I ever saw. See XVIIB (or - p.99)

Appendix A

The Alphabetical Homonym Index
(Simple Roots)

A (14 homonyms)
aid	(n-v)	p. 8
aide	(n)	p. 8
ail	(v)	p. 8
air	(n-v)	p. 8
all	(pro)	p.86
ale	(n)	p. 1
ant	(n)	p.14
arc	(n-v)	p.92
ark	(n)	p.92
ate	(v)	p. 1
aught	(n)	p.85
aunt	(n)	p.20
awl	(n)	p.87
aye	(n)	p.46

B (106 homonyms)
bach	(v)	p.14
bade	(v)	p. 1
bail	(n-v)	p. 8
bait	(n-v)	p. 8
bale	(n-v)	p. 1
bald	(adj)	p.87
ball	(n)	p.87
band	(n-v)	p.14
banned*	(v)	p.14
banns*	(n)	p.14
bans*	(n-v)	p.14
bard	(n-v)	p.92
bark	(n-v)	p.92
barque	(n)	p.92
barred*	(v)	p.92
bare	(v-adj-adv)	p. 2
base	(n-v)	p. 2
based*	(v)	p. 2
bass	(n)	p. 13
baste	(v)	p. 2
batch	(n)	p.14
bate	(v)	p. 2
bawl	(v)	p.87
bawled*	(v)	p.87
bay	(n-v)	p.10
bayed*	(v)	p.10
be	(v)	p.33
Bea	(n)	p.28
beach	(n-v)	p.28
bean	(n)	p.28
bear	(n)	p.12
beat	(n-v)	p.28
beau	(n)	p.65
bee	(n)	p.21
beech	(n)	p.21
been [1] [2]	(v)	p.47,21
beer	(n)	p.22
beet	(n)	p.22
bell	(n-v)	p.34
belle	(n)	p.34
berth	(n-v)	p.100
bey	(n)	p.12
bib	(n-v)	p.47
bibb	(n)	p.47
bier	(n)	p.32
bight	(n-v)	p.42
billed*	(v)	p.47
bin	(n-v)	p.47
bird	(n)	p.103
birl	(n-v)	p.103

107

birr	(n)	p.103	*breech*	(n-v)	p.22
birth	(n-v)	p.103	*brewed**	(v)	p.79
bit	(n-v)	p.47	*brews**	(n-v)	p.82
bite	(n-v)	p.37	*brood*	(n-v)	p.75
blessed*	(v)	p.34	*browse*	(v)	p.91
blest	(v)	p.34	*brows**	(n)	p.91
blew	(v)	p.79	*bruit*	(n-v)	p.82
blight	(n-v)	p.42	*bruise*	(n-v)	p.82
blite	(n-v)	p.37	*brute*	(n-adj)	p.82
bloc	(n)	p.66	*build*	(n-v)	p.47
block	(n-v)	p.65	*buoy²*	(n-v)	p.89
blue	(n-v-adj)	p.81	*bur*	(n)	p.105
bo	(n)	p.59	*burg*	(n)	p.105
boar	(n)	p.95	*burgh*	(n)	p.105
board	(n-v)	p.95	*burl*	(n-v)	p.105
bode	(v)	p.54	*burr*	(n-v)	p.103
bold	(adj)	p.60	*burred**	(v)	p.105
bole	(n)	p.54	*bus*	(n-v)	p.71
boll	(n-adj)	p.60	*buss*	(n-v)	p.71
bomb	(n-v)	p.66	*bussed**	(v)	p.71
bombe	(n)	p.66	*bust*	(n-v)	p.71
boos*	(n-v)	p.75	*but*	(conj)	p.71
booze	(n-v)	p.75	*butt*	(n-v)	p.71
bore	(n-v)	p.95	*buy*	(n-v)	p.46
bored*	(n)	p.94	*by*	(prep)	p.45
bough	(n)	p.90	*bye*	(n)	p.45
bow	(n-v)	p.60,90			
bowed*	(v)	p.54	**C** (102 homonyms)		
bowl	(n-v)	p.54	*cache*	(n-v)	p.15
bowled*	(v)	p.60	*Cain*	(n)	p. 8
boy	(n)	p.89	*calk*	(n-v)	p.87
braid	(n-v)	p. 8	*call*	(n-v)	p.87
braise	(v)	p. 8	*cane*	(n-v)	p. 2
brake	(n-v)	p. 1	*cant*	(n-v)	p.15
brayed*	(v)	p.10	*can't*	(contra)	p.15
brays*	(v)	p.10	*cash*	(n-v)	p.15
breach	(n-v)	p.28	*cast*	(n-v)	p.15
bread	(n-v)	p.36	*caste*	(n)	p.15
break	(n-v)	p.12	*caul*	(n)	p.85
bred	(v)	p.34	*caulk*	(n-v)	p.85

cause	(n-v)	p.85	coal	(n-v)	p.61
caws*	(n-v)	p.87	coaled	(v)	p.61
cay	(n)	p.10	coarse	(adj)	p.96
cede	(v)	p.31	coat	(n-v)	p.62
ceil	(v)	p.32	coax	(v)	p.62
cell	(n)	p.34	cocks*	(n-v)	p.66
cent	(n)	p.34	coin	(n-v)	p.88
cents*	(n)	p.35	cokes*	(n-v)	p.55
cere	(v)	p.102	cold	(n-adj)	p.60
cete	(n)	p.31	cole	(n)	p.55
chard	(n)	p.92	come	(v)	p.74
charred*	(v)	p.92	conch	(n)	p.66
chased*	(v)	p. 2	conk	(n-v)	p.66
chaste	(adj)	p. 2	coop	(n-v)	p.76
cheap	(adj)	p.22	copped*	(v)	p.66
check	(n-v)	p.35	cops*	(n)	p.66
cheep	(n-v)	p.22	copse	(n)	p.66
chews*	(n-v)	p.79	Copt	(n)	p.66
chic	(n-adj)	p.33	cord	(n-v)	p.94
chime	(n-v)	p.37	core	(n-v)	p.97
choir	(n-v)	p.46	cored	(v)	p.96
choose	(v)	p.76	corps	(n)	p.94
chord	(n-v)	p.94	corse	(n)	p.94
chute	(n)	p.82	cote	(n)	p.55
chyme	(n)	p.44	coupe	(n)	p.81
cinque	(n)	p.47	course	(n-v)	p.98
cist	(n)	p.48	cox	(n)	p.66
cite	(v)	p.38	creak	(n-v)	p.28
clack	(n-v)	p.15	creek	(n)	p.22
claque	(n)	p.15	crewed*	(v)	p.79
clause	(n)	p.86	crews*	(n-v)	p.79
claws*	(n-v)	p.87	cruise	(n-v)	p.82
cleek	(n)	p.22	crude	(adj)	p.82
clew	(n-v)	p.79	cruse	(n)	p.82
climb	(n-v)	p.38	cue	(n-v)	p.69
clime	(n)	p.38	cum	(prep)	p.72
clique	(n)	p.22	curt	(adj)	p.105
close	(v)	p.55	cyst	(n)	p.53
clothes*	(n)	p.55	czar	(n)	p.93
clue	(n-v)	p.79	Czech	(n)	p.35

D (29 homonyms)

dame	(n-v)	p.15
damn	(n-v)	p.15
Dane	(n)	p. 2
days*	(n)	p.10
daze	(n-v)	p. 2
draft	(n-v)	p.15
draught	(n)	p.20
deal	(n-v)	p.28
dear	(n-adj)	p.29
deer	(n)	p.22
deign	(v)	p.12
dele	(n-v)	p.31
dew	(n-v)	p.79
die	(n-v)	p.44
dine	(v)	p.38
do	(n-v)	p.60,83
doe	(n)	p.62
does	(n)	p.63
done	(v)	p.74
dor	(n)	p.94
door	(n)	p.98
dough	(n)	p.64
doze	(n-v)	p.55
ducked*	(v)	p.72
duct	(n)	p.72
due	(n-adj)	p.81
dun	(v)	p.72
dye	(n-v)	p.45
dyne	(n)	p.44

E (7 homonyms)

earn	(v)	p.101
eave	(n)	p.29
eight	(n)	p.12
ere	(prep)	p.13
eve	(n)	p.31
ewe	(n)	p.70
eye	(n-v)	p.46

F (53 homonyms)

fail	(v)	p. 8
faille	(n)	p. 8
fain	(adj)	p.12
faint	(n-v)	p. 8
fair	(n-adv)	p. 3
fare	(n-v)	p. 3
faze	(v)	p. 3
fay	(n-v)	p.10
feat	(n)	p.29
feed	(v)	p.22
feed*	(v)	p.22
fees*	(n-v)	p.23
feet	(n)	p.22
feeze	(v)	p.23
feign	(v)	p.12
feint	(n-v)	p.12
fey	(adj)	p.12
fined*	(v)	p.38
find	(n-v)	p.42
fir	(n)	p.103
fizz	(n-v)	p.48
flair	(n)	p. 8
flare	(n-v)	p. 3
flea	(n)	p.29
flecks*	(n-v)	p.35
flee	(v)	p.23
flew	(v)	p.80
flex	(v)	p.35
flocks	(n-v)	p.66
floe	(n)	p.63
flour	(n-v)	p.90
flower*	(n-v)	p.90
flu	(n)	p83
flue	(n)	p.81
foaled*	(v)	p.62
fold	(n-v)	p.60
for	(prep)	p.94
fore	(n-interj)	p.97

110

fort	(n)	p.94	graft	(n-v)	p.16
forte	(n)	p.95	graphed*	(v)	p.16
forth	(adv)	p.95	grate	(n)	p. 3
four	(adj)	p.97	gray	(adj)	p.10
fourth	(n-adj)	p.95	grays*	(n)	p.10
fraise	(n)	p. 8	graze	(v)	p. 3
franc	(n)	p.16	grease	(n-v)	p.23
frank	(n-v-adv)	p.16	great	(adj)	p.12
frays*	(n-v)	p.10	Greece	(n)	p.23
frees*	(v)	p.23	grey	(adj)	p.12
freeze	(n-v)	p.23	grill	(n-v)	p.48
frieze	(n)	p.32	grille	(n)	p.48
fur	(n-v)	p.105	grip	(n-v)	p.48
furs*	(n)	p.105	grippe	(n)	p.48
furze	(n)	p.105	groan	(n-v)	p.62
			grown	(v)	p.64

G (46 homonyms)

			guessed*	(v)	p.35
Gael	(n)	p.13	guest	(n)	p.35
gaff	(n-v)	p.16	guide	(n-v)	p.38
gaffe	(n)	p.16	guild	(n-v)	p.48
gage	(n)	p. 3	guilt	(n)	p.48
Gail	(n)	p. 8	guise	(n)	p.38
gait	(n)	p. 8	guyed*	(v)	p.46
gale	(adj)	p. 3	guys*	n-v)	p.46
gate	(n)	p. 3			
gauge	(n-v)	p.13			
gene	(n)	p.31	**H** (43 homonyms)		
gild	(v)	p.48	hail	(n-v-interj)	p. 8
gilt	(n-v)	p.48	hair	(n)	p. 9
glair	(n-v)	p. 8	hale	(v-adv)	p. 3
glare	(n-v)	p. 3	hall	(n)	p.87
gloom	(n-v)	p.76	hare	(n)	p. 3
glume	(n)	p.82	hart	(n)	p.93
gnat	(n)	p.16	haul	(n-v)	p.86
gnome	(n)	p.55	hay	(n-v)	p.10
gnu	(n)	p.83	hays*	(n-v)	p.10
gored	(v)	p.97	haze	(n-v)	p. 4
gourd	(n)	p.98	heal	(n-v)	p.29
gourde	(n)	p.98	hear	(v)	p.29

111

heard	(v)	p.101
heart	(n)	p.93
heel	(n-v)	p.23
heigh	(interj)	p.12
heir	(n)	p.12
herd	(n-v)	p.100
here	(adv)	p.32
hertz	(n)	p.100
hew	(v)	p.70
hey	(interj)	p.13
hi	(interj)	p.42
hide	(n-v)	p.38
hie	(v)	p.44
hied*	(v)	p.45
high	(adj)	p.42
higher	(adj)	p.42
hire	(v)	p.38
ho	(interj)	p.60
hoar	(n)	p.96
hoard	(n-v)	p.96
hoarse	(adj)	p.96
hoe	(n-v)	p.63
hoes*	(n-v)	p.63
hold	(n-v)	p.60
hole	(n-v)	p.56
holed*	(v)	p.56
horde	(n-v)	p.95
horse	(n-v)	p.95
hose	(n-v)	p.56
hour	(n)	p.90
hue	(n)	p.70
hurts*	(n-v)	p.105

I (6 homonyms)

I	(pro)	p.42
in	(prep)	p.48
inn	(n)	p.48
it's - it is	(contr)	p.49
it's - it has	(contr)	p.49
its	(pro)	p.49

J (6 homonyms)

jam	(n-v)	p.16
jamb	(n)	p.17
jean	(n)	p.29
Jean	(n)	p.29
jinks*	(n-v)	p.49
jinx	(n-v)	p.29

K (19 homonyms)

Kay	(n)	p.10
keel	(n-v)	p.23
Kiel	(n)	p.32
kill	(n-v)	p.49
kiln	(n-v)	p.49
knap	(n-v)	p.17
knave	(n)	p. 4
knead	(v)	p.29
knee	(n-v)	p.23
kneed	(v)	p.23
kneel	(v)	p.23
knew	(v)	p.80
knight	(n-v)	p.43
knit	(n-v)	p.49
knob	(n)	p.66
know	(v)	p.61
knows*	(v)	p.61
knot	(n-v)	p.67
kor	(n)	p.95

L (59 homonyms)

lacks*	(v)	p.17
lade	(v)	p. 4
laid	(v)	p. 9
lain	(v)	p. 9
lam	(n-v)	p.17
lamb	(n)	p.17
lane	(n)	p. 4
lap	(n-v)	p.17
Lapp	(n)	p.17

lax	(adj)	p.17	loon	(n)	p.76
laps*	(n-v)	p.17	loop	(n-v)	p.76
lapse	(n-v)	p.17	loot	(n-v)	p.76
lay	(n-v)	p.11	loupe	(n)	p.81
lays*	(n-v)	p.11	lowed*	(v)	p.64
laze	(v)	p. 4	lox	(n)	p.67
lea	(n)	p.29	lune	(n)	p.82
leach	(n-v)	p.29	lute	(n)	p.82
lead	(n)	p.36	lye	(n)	p.45
leaf	(n-v)	p.29	Lynn	(n)	p.53
leak	(n-v)	p.29	lynx	(n)	p.53
lean	(adj)	p.29			
Lear	(n)	p.29			
leased*	(v)	p.29	**M** (51 homonyms)		
least	(adj)	p.29	made	(v)	p. 4
led	(v)	p.35	maid	(n)	p. 9
lee	(adj)	p.24	mail	(n-v)	p. 9
leech	(n)	p.24	main	(adj)	p. 9
leek	(n)	p.24	maize	(n)	p. 9
leer	(n-v)	p.24	male	(n)	p. 4
lei	(n)	p.12	mall	(n)	p.87
let	(v)	p.35	mane	(n)	p. 4
Lett	(n)	p.35	marc	(n)	p.93
ley	(n)	p.13	mark	(n-v)	p.93
lie	(n-v)	p.45	massed*	(v)	p.17
lief	(adv)	p.32	mast	(n)	p.17
lien	(n)	p.32	mat	(n-v)	p.18
lieu	(n)	p.83	matte	(n-v)	p.18
limb	(n-v)	p.49	maul	(n-v)	p.86
limn	(n)	p.49	maze	(n)	p. 4
lin	(n)	p.49	mead	(n)	p.29
linn	(n)	p.49	mean	(adj-v)	p.30
links*	(n-v)	p.53	meat	(n)	p.30
load	(n-v)	p.62	Mede	(n)	p.32
loan	(n-v)	p.62	meet	(n-v)	p.24
locks*	(n-v)	p.69	mete	(v)	p.32
lode	(n)	p.56	mewl	(n-v)	p.70
lone	(adj)	p.56	mews*	(n-v)	p.70
loo	(n)	p.76	mien	(n)	p.32

might	(n-v)	p.43		*nit*	(n)	p.50
mil	(n)	p.50		*no*	(adv)	p.61
mill	(n-v)	p.50		*nob*	(n)	p.67
mind	(n-v)	p.43		*nock*	(n-v)	p.67
mined*	(v)	p.38		*Noh*	(n)	p.65
minks*	(n)	p.50		*nome*	(n)	p.65
minx	(n)	p.50		*Nome*	(n)	p.56
missed*	(v)	p.50		*none*	(pro)	p.74
mist	(n-v)	p.50		*nos**	(n)	p.61
mite	(n)	p.38		*nose*	(n-v)	p.57
moan	(n-v)	p.62		*not*	(adv)	p.67
moat	(n-v)	p.62		*nun*	(n)	p.72
mode	(n)	p.56				
mood	(n)	p.77		**O** (10 homonyms)		
mooed*	(v)	p.77		*oar*	(n-v)	p.97
morn	(n)	p.95		*ode*	(n)	p.57
mot	(n)	p.60		*oh*	(interj)	p.65
mote	(n)	p.56		*one*	(adj)	p.74
mourn	(v)	p.98		*or*	(conj)	p.95
mow	(n-v)	p.64		*ore*	(n)	p.97
mowed*	(v)	p.64		*ought*	(v)	p.87
mown	(v-adj)	p.64		*our*	(pro)	p.91
mule	(n)	p.69		*owe*	(v)	p.65
muse	(n-v)	p.69		*owed*	(v)	p.64
mussed*	(v)	p.72				
must	(v)	p.72		**P** (72 homonyms)		
				paced*	(v)	p. 4
N (23 homonyms)				*packed**	(v)	p.18
nave	(n)	p. 4		*pact*	(n)	p.18
nap	(n)	p.18		*pail*	(n)	p. 9
nappe	(n)	p.18		*pain*	(n-v)	p. 9
nay	(n)	p.11		*pair*	(n-v)	p. 9
nee[1]	(adj)	p.13		*pale*	(adj)	p. 4
nee[2]	(adj)	p.24		*pall*	(n)	p.87
need	(n-v)	p.24		*pan*	(n-v)	p.18
neigh	(n-v)	p.12		*pane*	(n	p. 4
Neil	(n)	p.32		*panne*	(n)	p.18
new	(adj)	p.80		*par*	(n)	p.93
night	(n)	p.43				

pard	(n)	p.93			
pare	(v)	p. 4	plait	(n-v)	p. 9
parr	(n)	p.93	plane	(n)	p. 5
parred*	(v)	p.93	plate	(n-v)	p. 5
passed*	(v)	p.18	pleas*	(n)	p.30
past	(adv)	p.18	please	(v)	p.30
paste	(n-v)	p. 5	plum	(n)	p.72
Paul	(n)	p.87	plumb	(n-v)	p.72
pause	(n-v)	p.86	pocks*	(n)	p.67
paws*	(n-v)	p.87	poem	(n)	p.57
pawl	(n)	p.87	pole	(n-v)	p.57
pea	(n)	p.30	poll	(n-v)	p.61
peace	(n)	p.30	pome	(n)	p.57
peak	(n-v)	p.30	pool	(n-v)	p.77
peal	(n-v)	p.30	pox	(n)	p.67
pear	(n)	p.12	praise	(n-v)	p. 9
pearl	(n)	p.101	pray	(v)	p.11
peat	(n)	p.30	prays*	(v)	p.11
pee	(n-v)	p.24	prey	(n)	p.13
peek	(n-v)	p.25	pride	(n-v)	p.39
peel	(n-v)	p.25	pried*	(v)	p.45,46
peer	(n-v)	p.25	pries*	(v)	p.45,46
per	(prep)	p.100	prince	(n)	p.50
Pete	(n)	p.32	prints*	(n-v)	p.50
phase	(n)	p. 5	prize	(n-v)	p.39
phiz	(n)	p.50	pros*	(n)	p.61
phlox	(n)	p.67	prose	(n-v)	p.57
phrase	(n-v)	p. 5	psi ^{2}	(n)	p.43
pi	(n)	p.43	pul	(n)	p.83
picked*	(v)	p.50	purl	(n-v)	p.105
picks*	(n)	p.53	pyx	(n)	p.53
Pict	(n)	p.50			
pie	(n)	p.45	**Q** (7 homonyms)		
piece	(n-v)	p.32	quarts*	(n)	p.98
pier	(n)	p.32	quartz	(n)	p.98
pique	(n-v)	p.33	quean	(n)	p.30
pix	(n)	p.53	queen	(n)	p.25
place	(n-v)	p. 5	queue	(n-v)	p.70
plaice	(n)	p. 9	quire	(n-v)	p.39
plain	(n)	p. 9	quoin	(n-v)	p.88

R (67 homonyms)

rack	(n-v)	p.18
rail	(n-v)	p. 9
rain	(n-v)	p. 9
raise	(v)	p. 9
rale	(n)	p. 5
rap	(n-v)	p.18
rapped*	(v)	p.19
rapt	(adj)	p.19
rays*	(n)	p.11
raze	(v)	p. 6
read	(v)	p.30,36
real	(adj)	p.25
red	(n)	p.35
reed	(n)	p.25
reek	(n-v)	p.25
reel	(n-v)	p.25
rein	(n)	p.12
reign	(n-v)	p.12
rest	(n)	p.35
retch	(v)	p.35
rheum	(n)	p.83
rhumb	(n)	p.73
rhyme	(n-v)	p.44
riel	(n)	p.32
riffed*	(v)	p.50
rift	(n-v)	p.51
right	(n-adj)	p.43
rime	(n-v)	p.39
rind	(n)	p.43
ring	(n-v)	p.51
rite	(n)	p.39
road	(n)	p.62
roam	(v)	p.62
rode	(v)	p.57
roe	(n)	p.63
roil	(v)	p.88
role	(n)	p.58
roll	(n-v)	p.61
Rome	(n)	p.58
rood	(n)	p.77
room	(n-v)	p.77
root	(n-v)	p.77
rose	(n-v)	p.58
rote	(n-adj)	p.58
rough	(n-v-adj)	p.75
rouse	(n-v)	p.91
rout	(n-v)	p.91
route^1	(n-v)	p.81
route^2	(n-v)	p.91
roux	(n)	p.81
rouxs*	(n)	p.81
row^1	(n-v)	p.64
rows*^{1}	(n-v)	p.64
rows*^{2}	(n-v)	p.91
rowed*^{1}	(v)	p.64
royal	(n-adj)	p.88
rude	(adj)	p.82
rue	(n-v)	p.81
rued*	(v)	p.81
rues*	(v)	p.81
ruff	(n-v)	p.72
rum	(n)	p.73
rung	(n-v)	p.73
ruse	(n)	p.82
rye	(n)	p.45
rynd	(n)	p.46

S (114 homonyms)

sac	(n)	p.19
sack	(n-v)	p.19
sail	(n-v)	p. 9
sale	(n)	p. 6
scat	(v)	p.19
scene	(n)	p.32
scull	(n-v)	p.73
sea	(n)	p.30
seal	(n-v)	p.30

seam	(n-v)	p.30	site	(n)	p.40
sear	(n-v)	p.30	size	(n-v)	p.40
seas*	(n)	p.30	skat	(v)	p.19
seat	(n-v)	p.30	skull	(n-adj)	p.73
see	(n-v)	p.26	slay	(v)	p.11
seed	(n-v)	p.26	sleave	(n-v)	p.30
seek	(v)	p.26	sleeve	(n-v)	p.27
seem	(v)	p.26	sleigh	(n-v)	p.12
seen	(v)	p.26	sleight	(n)	p.46
sees*	(v)	p.26	slew	(n-v)	p.80
seize	(v)	p.32	slight	(n-v-adj)	p.43
sense	(n-v)	p.36	sloe	(n)	p.63
sere	(adj)	p.32	slow	(v-adj)	p.64
serf	(n)	p.100	slue	(n-v)	p.80
serge	(n)	p.101	so	(adv)	p.61
sew	(v)	p.65	soak	(n-v)	p.62
sewn	(v)	p.65	soar	(n-v)	p.97
shake	(n-v)	p. 6	soke	(n)	p.58
shear	(v)	p.30	sold	(v)	p.61
sheer	(v-adj)	p.26	sole	(n-v)	p.58
sheik[1]	(n)	p.33	soled*	(v)	p.59
sheik[2]	(n)	p.12	some	(adj)	p.74
shoe	(n-v)	p.83	son	(n)	p.74
shoo	(interj)	p.77	sone	(n)	p.59
shoot	(n-v)	p.77	soot[2]	(n)	p.78
shot	(n-v)	p.67	sord	(n)	p.95
shott	(n)	p.67	sore	(n-adj)	p.97
sic	(v-adv)	p.51	sough[2]	(v)	p.91
sick	(adj)	p.51	soul	(n)	p.64
side	(n-v)	p.39	sow[1]	(v)	p.64
sigh	(n-v)	p.43	sow[2]	(n)	p.91
sighed*	(v)	p.43	sown	(v)	p.64
sighs*	(v)	p.43	spade	(n)	p. 6
sight	(n-v)	p.43	spayed*	(v)	p.11
sign	(n-v)	p.43	spice	(n-v)	p.40
Sikh	(n)	p.33	spright	(n)	p.43
sine	(n)	p.40	sprite	(n)	p.40
sink	(n-v)	p.51	staff	(n-v)	p.19
Sioux	(n)	p.81	staid	(adj)	p. 9
sir	(n)	p.104	stair	(n)	p. 9

stake	(n-v)	p. 6	tail	(n-v)	p. 9
staph	(adj)	p.19	tale	(n)	p. 6
stare	(n-v)	p. 6	tale	(n)	p. 6
stayed*	(v)	p.11	tare	(n)	p. 6
steak	(n)	p.12	taught	(v)	p.86
steal	(n-v)	p.30	taught	(v)	p.86
steel	(n)	p.27	taut	(adj)	p.86
steer	(n-v)	p.27	tax	(n-v)	p.19
steeve	(n-v)	p.27	tea	(n)	p.30
stere	(n)	p.32	team	(n-v)	p.30
Steve	(n)	p.32	tear	(n-v)	p.12,31
stich	(n-v)	p.51	teas*	(n)	p.31
sticks*	(n-v)	p.51	tease	(n-v)	p.31
stile	(n)	p.40	tee	(n-v)	p.27
stitch	(n-v)	p.51	teem	(v)	p.27
stoop	(n-v)	p.78	terce	(n)	p.101
straight	(adj-adv)	p. 9	tern	(n)	p.101
strait	(n)	p. 9	terse	(adj)	p.101
stupe	(n)	p.82	their	(pro)	p.12
style	(n-v)	p.44	there	(adv)	p.13
Styx	(n)	p.53	they're	(contr)	p.13
sue	(v)	p.81	threw	(v)	p.80
suede	(adj)	p.13	throe	(n)	p.63
suit	(n-v)	p.83	throne	(n-v)	p.59
suite	(n)	p.27	through	(prep)	p.81
sum	(n-v)	p.73	throw	(n-v)	p.64
sun	(n-v)	p.73	thrown	(v)	p.64
surf	(n-v)	p.105	thyme	(n)	p.44
surge	(n-v)	p.105	tic	(n)	p.52
swayed*	(v)	p.11	tick	(n-v)	p.52
sweet	(adj)	p.27	tide	(n-v)	p.41
sword	(n)	p.95	tied*	(v)	p.45
sync	(n-v)	p.53	tier	(n-v)	p.32
			tierce	(n)	p.102
T (78 homonyms)			time	(n-v)	p.41
tacked*	(v)	p.19	tine	(n)	p.41
tacks*	(n-v)	p.19	tire	(n-v)	p.41
tact	(n)	p.19	to	(inf-prep)	p.83
tael	(n)	p.13	toad	(n)	p.62

toe	(n-v)	p.63
toed*	(n-adj)	p.63
told	(v)	p.61
tole	(n)	p.59
toll	n)	p.61
tolled*	(v)	p.61
ton	(n)	p.74
too	(adv)	p.78
tool	(n-v)	p.78
toon	(n)	p.78
tor	(n)	p.95
tore	(v)	p.97
torr	(n)	p.98
tough	(n-adj)	p.75
tow	(n-v)	p.64
towed*	(v)	p.64
tracked*	(v)	p.19
tract	(n)	p.19
tray	(n)	p.11
trey	(n)	p.13
troop	(n-v)	p.79
troupe	(n-v)	p.81
trussed*	v)	p.73
trust	(n-v)	p.74
tsar	(n)	p.93
tuff	(n)	p.74
tulle	(n)	p.82
tun	(n)	p.74
tune[1]	(n-v)	p.82
turn	9n-v)	p.105
twerp	(n)	p.101
twirp	(n)	p.104
two	(adj)	p.83
Tyne	(n)	p.44
Tyre	(n)	p.44

<u>U</u> (1 homonym)

urn	(n)	p.105

<u>V</u> (8 homonyms)

vail	(v)	p. 9
vain	(n-adj)	p. 9
vale	(n)	p. 6
vane	(n)	p. 7
veil	(n)	p.12
vein	(n)	p.12
vice	(n-adj)	p.41
vise	(n-v)	p.41

<u>W</u> (109 homonyms)

waffed*	(v)	p.20
waft[2]	(n-v)	p.20
wail	(n-v)	p. 9
wain	(n)	p.10
waist	(n)	p.10
wait	(n-v)	p.10
waive	(v)	p.10
wale	(n)	p. 7
wand	(n)	p.68
wane	(v)	p. 7
wanned*	(v)	p.68
war	(n-v)	p.98
ware	(n)	p. 7
wart	(n)	p.98
waste	(n-v)	p. 7
watt	(n)	p.68
wave	(n-v)	p. 7
wax	(n-v)	p.20
way	(n)	p.11
Wayne	(n)	p. 7
we	(pro)	p.33
weak	(adj)	p.31
weal	(n)	p.31

weald	(n)	p.31	whop	(n-v)	p.68
wean	(v)	p.31	whore	(n-v)	p.97
wear	(n-v)	p.12	whored*	(v)	p.95
weave	(n-v)	p.31	whorl	(n)	p.99
wee	(adj)	p.28	whys*	(n)	p.46
week	(n)	p.28	wield	(v)	p.32
ween	(v)	p.28	wig	(n-v)	p.52
weigh	(v)	p.12	wight	(n-adj)	p.43
weight	(n)	p.12	wild	(n-adj)	p.43
weir	(n)	p.33	wile	(n-v)	p.42
wen	(n)	p.36	wiled*	(v)	p.42
were	(v)	p.102	win	(n-v)	p.52
we're - we were (contr)		p.33	wind	(n-v)	p.44,52
wet	(v-adj)	p.36	wine	(n-v)	p.42
we've - we have (contr)		p.33	wined*	(v)	p.42
whacks*	(n-v)	p.20	wise	(n-adj)	p.42
whale	(n)	p. 7	wit	(n)	p.52
what	(pro)	p.68	witch	(n-v)	p.52
wheal	(n)	p.31	with	(prep)	p.52
wheel	(n-v)	p.28	withe	(n-v)	p.52
wheeled*	(v)	p.28	woe	(n)	p.64
when	(adv)	p.36	won	(v)	p.74
where	(adv)	p.13	wood	(n-v)	p.84
whet	(v)	p.36	wop	(n)	p.68
whey	(n)	p.13	word	(n-v)	p.99
which	(pro)	p.52	wore	(v)	p.97
Whig	(n)	p.52	world	(n)	p.99
while	(n-v-conj)	p.41	wort [2]	(n)	p.95
whiled*	(v)	p.41	worst	(adj)	p.99
whine	(n-v)	p.41	would	(v)	p.84
whined*	(v)	p.41	wrack	(n)	p.20
whir	(n-v)	p.104	wrap	(n-v)	p.20
whirl	(n-v)	p.104	wrapped*	(v)	p.20
whirled*	(v)	p.104	wrath	(n)	p.20
whirred*	(v)	p.104	wreak	(v)	p.31
whit	(n)	p.52	wreck	(n-v)	p.36
white	(n-adj)	p.42	wrest	(v)	p.36
whoa	(interj)	p.62	wretch	(n)	p.36
whole	(n-adj)	p.59	wright	(n)	p.44

wring	(v)	p.52
write	(v)	p.42
wrote	(v)	p.59
wrung	(v)	p.74
wry	(adj)	p.46
wurst	(n)	p.105
wynd	(n)	p.53
wynn	(n)	p.53

X (1 homonym)
| xu | (n) | p.83 |

Y (4 homonyms)
yew	(n)	p.70,80
yoke	(n-v)	p.59
yolk	(n)	p.61
you	(pro)	p.70,80

Z (1 homonym)
| zoo | (n) | p.79 |

* A simple root with an inflection.

Addenda
reck	(v)	p.35
seise	(v)	p.32
wade -	(v)	See *weighed** p.12

weighed* (v) See p.12

ward - *We lived in a small city* **ward** (n). or *The hospital* **ward** (n) *was small.* or *She is a* **ward** (n) *of the court.* or *The serum will help to* **ward** (v) *off the disease.*
  Also: **warred***(v) - *We* **warred** *with the enemy constantly.*

Appendix B

The Polysyllabic Homonym Index
(Complex roots)

ado - *There was much **ado** about the accident.*
adieu - *I bid you a fond **adieu**.* (Secondary pronunciation)
aisle - *The usher led us down the **aisle**.* (See **isle**)
altar - *The sacrifice was placed on the **altar**.*
alter - *If I **alter** the house, it will look better.*
aster - *An **aster** is a flower; it is also a term used biology.*
Astor - *John Jacob **Astor** was a fur trader.*
auger - *An **auger** is a large boring tool.*
augur - *An **augur** is a prophet or seer.* <u>or</u> *The old man could **augur** the future by using signs.*
aural - *His **aural** (ear)canals were blocked.* (See **oral**)
baron - *The term **baron** is one referring to heditary titles.*
barren - *A word used to describe sterility or childlessness.*
better - *I feel **better** today than I did yesterday.*
bettor - *A **bettor** is a person whobets.* (Also better)
bridal - *The young woman had a **bridal** party.*
bridle - *Who can put a **bridle** on the wild horse?*
buccal - *The man had a **buccal** (mouth cavity) problem.*
buckle - *Where is the new **buckle** for my jacket?*<u>or</u> *Will he **buckle** (collapse) under pressure?*
berry - *A **berry** is a fleshy, edible fruit.* (See **bury**)
burro - *A **burro** is a small pack animal.*
borough - *A **borough** is a self-governing entity.*
burrow - *The rabbit lived in a **burrow**.* <u>or</u> *He will **burrow** into the hillside.*
bury - *They will **bury** the body tomorrow.* (See **berry**)
caddie - *My **caddie** lost my clubs and my golf balls.*
caddy - *The small **caddy** held the tea very nicely.*
callous - *He is a very **callous** (insensitive) fellow.*
callus - *How did the man get that large **callus** on his hand?*
cannon - *The **cannon** fired many shells.* <u>or</u> *The **cannon** is also the name of a bone in a horse's leg.* <u>or</u> *They will begin to **cannon** (commence firing) soon.*
canon - *An ecclesiastical, or secular, law or code of laws.*
canter - *His horse moved at a **canter** (a slow gait).*

cantor - A *cantor* is a special singer in a synagogue.
canvas - All the tents were made of *canvas*.
canvass - The salesmen went to *canvass* (solicit) the neighborhood for customers.
capital - The *capital* is a major city serving as the seat of government. or Dad loaned me some money to use as *capital* for my new business.
capitol - The *capitol* is a building where official governmental bodies convene.
carat - She wore a one *carat* diamond. (See *carrot*)
caret - A *caret* is a proofreading symbol used to indicate where a thing is to be inserted in a line of printed matter.
Note - Although the final syllable in *caret* is properly pronounced as (kar' it), rather than with the sound of the *schwa* (ə), as it is in *carat*, *carrot*, and *karat* (kar'ə t), hearing such a minisicule difference is very difficult and leads to considerable confusion. In the few homonyms where confusion may exist, the reader will be referred to this Note for clarification concerning the role of the *schwa* in final syllables.
carol - The choir sang a joyous *carol* today. (See *carrel*)
carrel - A *carrel* is a library nook used for private study.
carrot - A *carrot* is an edible root vegetable. (See *carat*)
caster - A *caster* is one who casts; is is also a small wheel on a swivel placed under heavy objects to make them easy to move.
castor - *Castor* is a substance used in the making of perfume, lubricants, and cathartics; it is also a a fabric. or *Castor* is also the name of one of the twin sons of Leda in Greek Mythology, or of a twin star in Gemini.
cellar - The furnace is down in the *cellar*. (See *seller*)
caudal - The *caudal* (posterior) fin was damaged.
caudle - *Caudle* is a warm drink given to the sick.
censer - A *censer* is a vessel for incense. (See *senser*)
censor - A *censor* is a person who examines mail, literature, art, etc. and makes a judgement about its propriety. To perform such activity is to *censor*.
center - The telsescope was aimed at the *center*. or The *center* snaps the football over my head. (See *scenter*)
cereal - The children ate *cereal* for breakfast. (See *serial*)

choler[1] - (Archaic) *In the Middle Ages, a choler was one of the four humors of the body thought to cause bad temper or anger.* (See **collar**)
choler[2] - Same definition as **choler**[1] (See **coaler**)
choral - *I like to listen to choral music.* (See **coral**)
coaler - *We loaded coal on a large coaler.* (See **choler**[2])
coco - *A coconut grows on a coco tree.*
cocoa - *Cocoa is a beverage made from cacao seeds.*
collar - *The collar on my shirt was torn.* (See **choler**[1])
colonel - *Uncle Rich was once a colonel in the U.S. Army.* (See **kernel**)
coral - *We found beautiful coral on the reef.* (See **choral**)
corbeil - *A corbeil is a scuptured basket of fruits or flowers used as an architectural ornament.*
corbel[1] - *A corbel is a bracket of stone or wood used to support a cornice or an arch.*
cruel - *Joseph is a very cruel person.*
crewel - *Crewel is a type of yarn used in embroidery.*
currant - *A currant is a small, sour fruit that grows on a prickly bush.*
current - *The river current was very rapid.* or *The current cost of fuel was high.*
cymbal - *A cymbal is a brass plate which is sounded by being struck by a drumstick.* (See **symbol**)
dinkey - (Informal) *A dinkey is a small locomotive.*
dinky - (Informal) *He gave me a dinky (small) portion.*
discreet - *His behavior was very discreet.*
discrete - *A discrete thing is one which is distinct.*
disgust - *The ugliness of the place filled me with disgust.*
discussed - *Tom and I discussed the whole situation.*
docile - *The docile tiger was submissive.* (See **dossal**)
dolman - *A dolman is a long cloak or coat with sleeves.*
dolmen - *A dolmen is a type of prehistoric stone structure.*
dossal - *A dossal is an ornamental fabric that hangs by an altar or a throne.* (See **docile**)
faker - *A faker is a person who acts in a misleading way.*
fakir[2] - *A fakir is a Moslem or Hindu mendicant.*
falter - *To falter means to waver or hesitate.* (See **faulter**)
fantom - Variant spelling of **phantom**.

faulter - A *faulter* is one who finds fault. (See **falter**)
ferret - A *ferret* is a domesticated polecat; it is also a narrow piece of tape used for binding fabric.
ferrite - A type of nonmetallic compound.
filum - A *filum* is an tanatomical structure. (See **phylum**)
frenzy - Variant spelling of **phrensy**.
fusil - A *fusil* is a light, flintlock musket.
fusile - The material was *fusile* (capable of being fused).
gallop - Will you *gallop* my horse for me?
galop - The *galop* was a lively 19th century dance.
gamble - He took a *gamble* on the horse. <u>or</u> Do you like to *gamble*?
gambol - I went for a *gambol* in the wood. <u>or</u> We like to *gambol* and frolic in the morning.
gimel - A *gimel* is the third letter of the Hebrew alphabet.
gimmal - A *gimmal* is a ring made of two narrower interlocked rings.
grisly - We went to a *grisly* (horrible) film.
grizzly - *Grizzly* means grayish. It is also part of the name for the *grizzly* bear.
hangar - Did he put the plane in the *hangar*?
hanger - She placed the coat on a *hanger*.
holy - The *holy* man was loved by all. (See **wholly**)
hostel - The campers stayed at the youth *hostel*.
hostile - Jim was very *hostile* toward his enemies.
idle - Because there was no work, the men were *idle*. <u>or</u> The motor will *idle* slowly.
idol - The people worshipped a false *idol*.
idyll - The poet wrote an *idyll* (a scene of rustic life).
isle - The boat landed at a small *isle*. (See **aisle**)
karat - A *karat* is a measure of gold. (See **carat**)
kernel - A *kernel* is a grain or seed of a cereal grass enclosed in a hard husk; it is also the inner core of a nut or pit which is usually edible. <u>or</u> The teacher had the *kernel* of a great idea. (See **colonel**)
levin - *Levin* is an archaic word for lightning.
leaven - *Leaven* is a substance used to ferment dough.
linen - The napkins were made of pure *linen*.
linin - *Linin* is a material found in the cell nucleus.
liar - A *liar* is a person who deliberately deceives.

lyre - *Mary learned to play the lyre* (stringed instrument).
mantel - *She put the dish on the mantel over the fireplace.*
mantle - *A mantle is a type of loose, sleeveless cloak.*
mackle - *A mackle is a blurred spot resulting from slipping print.* (Also **macule**)
macle - *Macle is the mineral chiastolite.*
marshall - *He had to marshal his troops.* (See **martial**)
marten - *The marten is a fur-bearing carnivore.*
martin - *The martin is a bird related to the swallow.*
martial - *Dick had a martial* (military) *look.* (See **marshal**)
maser - *A maser is a device used to convert electromagnetic radiation.*
mazer - *A mazer is a type of drinking bowl or goblet.*
medal - *The hero wore his medal proudly.*
meddle - *Why do you always meddle in my business?*
metal - *The cans were made of metal.*
mettle - *His mettle* (courage) *was tested in the battle.*
miner - *A miner is a person who works in a mine.* (See **minor**)
minor - *A minor is a person who is under lega;l age; it also refers to a thing which is lesser in size, weight, rank, etc.* (See **miner**)
missal - *A missal is a type of prayer book.*
missile - *The gunner fired the missile.*
mistle - Used only in **mistletoe** and **mistle thrush**.
morning - *I'll meet you tomorrow morning at ten.*
mourning - *The widow was dressed for mourning.*
muscle - *The muscle in my arm is sore.*
mussel - *A mussel is a marine bivalve mollusk.*
naval - *The battleship was sunk in a naval engagement.*
navel - *The mark on the abdomen of mammals where the umbilical cord is attached during gestation.*
oral - *The child had an oral* (spoken) *language problem.* (See **aural**)
parlay - *He is going to parlay* (bet) *his winnings and make a bet in the next game.*
parley - *Everyone came to the parley* (meeting) *late.*
pecten - *A pecten is a structure resembling a comb found in birds and reptiles.* (See **Note** with **caret**)
pectin - *A substance found in ripe fruit and used for jelling.*

pedal - The *pedal* on my bike broke. or Can you *pedal* faster?
peddle - The salesman goes up the road to *peddle* goods.
pekan - The *pekan* is mammal. (See **Note** with **caret**)
pekin - *Pekin* is a type of striped silk fabric.
pencel - A *pencel* is a kind of narrow banner carried on the top of a spear or lance.
pencil - Dad always uses a *pencil* to write notes.
petrel - The *petrel* is a type of sea bird.
petrol - (British) She put *petrol* (gasoline) in her car.
phantom - The *phantom* made a ghostly appearance. (See **fantom**)
phenol - A type of poisonous white crystalline compound.
phenyl - A *phenyl* results from the removal of hydrogen.
phrensy - They ran about in a wild *phrensy*.(See **frenzy**)
phylum - A *phylum* is a taxonomical division of the animal world. or It is also a large division of genetically related language families. (See **filum**)
pickle - Mom took a sour *pickle* from the barrel.
picul - A *picul* is a unit of weight used in the Far East.
pidgin - A simplified form of speech used for communication by groups speaking different languages.
pigeon - A *pigeon* is a common type of bird. or (Slang) The swindler was looking for a *pigeon* (dupe).
pistil - The *pistil* is the seed-bearing organ of a flower. (See **Note** with **caret**)
pistol - The lawman fired his *pistol* at the thief.
pleural - Jack had a type of *pleural* pneumonia.
plural - The word *plural* is used to designate more than one of a singular noun form.
presser - The *presser* ironed all of our clothes for us.
pressor - A *pressor* nerve creates increased activity.
prier - A *prier* is one who pries. (Also pryer)
principal - The *principal* led everyone from the school.
principle - A *principle* is a basic truth or law.
prior - I was late because I had a *prior* appointment. or A *prior* is a monastic officer in charge of a priory.
profit - Bill made a large *profit* from his investment.
prophet - The *prophet* spoke from divine inspiration.

psalter - A *psalter* is a book containing the Book of Psalms. (See **salter**)
rabbet - A *rabbet* is a groove near the edge of a piece of wood.
rabbit - The white *rabbit* went scurrying over the field.
raven - The *raven* is a large black bird. or Why did he *raven* (devour greedily) his food?
ravin - The eagle devoured his *ravin* (prey). (Also **raven**)
raiser - One who raises things is a *raiser*.
razor - A *razor* is a sharp edged cutting instrument.
receipt - Did you get a *receipt* with your purchase? (See **reseat**)
remand - The judge will *remand* him to jail.
remanned - The fort needed to be *remanned* (restaffed).
remind - Will you *remind* Tom to be on time?
remined - The old ore deposit was *remined*.
reseat - Where will he *reseat* the guests? (See **receipt**)
review - The teacher said she would *review* the material.
revue - The audience loved the new *revue* (show).
riband - (Archaic) A *riband* was a decorative ribbon.
ribband - A *ribband* is a length of wood or metal used in ship building.
rigger - A *rigger* is one who rigs, especially a ship's rigging or parachutes.
rigor - *Rigor* refers to strictness, severity, harshness, etc.
riot - The police were called to stop the *riot*. (See **ryot**)
roomer - A new *roomer* rents the apartment. (See **rumor**)
rowan - The *rowan* is a small deciduous tree.
rowen - A *rowen* is a second crop harvested in a season.
rumor - Patty spread a *rumor* that isn't true. (see **roomer**)
ryot - A *ryot* is a peasant farmer in India. (See **riot**)
sabbat - The name referred to as the witches' Sabbath.
sabot - A *sabot* is a tyoe of shoe or sandal.
sachet - A *sachet* is a small bag of scented powder used to scent clothes or closets. (See **sashay**)
salter - A *salter* is one who manufactures, or treats food with, salt. (See **psalter**)
sashay - (Informal) Let's *sashay* (strut) over to the club. (See **sachet**)
saver - One who saves is a *saver*.

savor - The *savor* is the quality of taste or aroma of a thing. or *To savor* is to taste or smell a thing.
scenter - A *scenter* is one who scents. (See **center**)
seller - I was the *seller;* he was the buyer. (See **cellar**)
senate - Mr. Smith was elected to serve in the *senate.*
sennet - A *sennet* is a type of barracuda.
sennit - *Sennit* is a type of nautical cordage.
seaman - A *seaman* is a sailor or man of the sea.
semen - A secretion of the male reproductive organ.
senser - One whose awareness comes from the senses is a *senser.* (See **censer**)
sensor - A *sensor* is a device that responds to signals.
serial - Are the *serial* numbers on the motor?(See **cereal**)
sewer - All the water drained into the *sewer.* (See **suer**)
spital - (Obsolete) *Spital* is an old name for a hospital.
spittle - Some *spittle* (saliva) dribbled from his mouth.
stabile - His condition remained *stabile* (unchanging). (See **Note** with **caret**)
stable - The horses were all placed in the *stable.* or *The substance is very stable.*
stolen - All of our money was *stolen.*
stollen - The baker made a *stollen* (a rich yeast cake).
stolon - A *stolon* [2] is a type of stem.
succor - They gave *succor* (aid) to their friends in need.
sucker - That *sucker* (foolish person) lost all his money.
suer - One who sues another is called a *suer.* (See **sewer**)
symbol - A *symbol* is something that represents something else by association or resemblance, as a musical sign, or a flag to stand for a country. (See **cymbal**)
taper - A *taper* is a slender candle. or *To taper* means to become gradually narrower.
tapir - A *tapir* is a heavy-bodied mammal with short legs and a fleshy proboscis(nose).
tenace [3] - A *tenace* is a combination of high cards in a player's hand in bridge or whist. (See **tennis**)
tenner - (Slang) I won a *tenner* (a ten dolar bill) on the big race. (See **tenor**)
tennis - We play *tennis* twice each week.(See **tenace**[3])
tenor - The *tenor* of the conversation was grim. or *The tenor* had a powerful voice. (See **tenner**)

tighter - *His grip got tighter as the man struggled.* (See **titer**)
timbal - *A timbal is a kettledrum.* (Also **tymbal**)
timbale - *A timbale is a custardlike dish of cheese, chicken, fish, vegetables, etc., and baked in a pastry mold.*
timber - *The man cut all the timber from the land.*
timbre - *The timbre* (quality of sound) *of the violin was beautiful to hear.*
titer - *Titer refers to the concentration of a substance in solution.* (Also **titre**) (See **tighter**)
tooter - *A tooter is a type of whistle.*
tutor - *My tutor taught me to speak three languages.*
tracter - *A tracter is one who writes tracts* (religious pamphlets).
tractor - *He sat on the tractor as it pulled the heavy load.*
troche - *A troche is a small medicinal lozenge.*
trochee - *A trochee is a measurement used in prosody.*
turban - *A turban is a type of Moslem headdress.*
turbine [1] - *A turbine is a type of machine.* (See **Note** with **caret**)
turbit - *A turbit is a breed of domestic pigeon.* (See **Note** with **caret**)
turbot - *The turbot is a European flatfish.*
villain - *When the villain was on the screen, we booed.*
villein - *A villein was a feudal serf with special status.*
villous - *The villous plant was covered with villi* (unmatted hairs).
villus - *A villus is a hairlike outgrowth; it is also a minute projection on a mucous membrane.*
weather - *The weather was cold, wet, and damp.*
wether - *A wether is a gelded male sheep.*
whether - *I don't care whether or not they come to visit.*
whither - *Whither are we going?* or *Whither the road goes, so go I.* (See **wither**)
wholly - *His story was not wholly true.* (See **holy**)
wither - *The frost caused the fruit to wither on the vine.* (See **whither**)

Total Complex Homonym Count - 269

Appendix C

The Quantitative Homonym Index
(Simple roots)

		Homonym Total
I	The Long Vowel Sound of A	171
II	The Short Vowel Sound of A	71
III	The Long Vowel Sound of E	145
IV	The Short Vowel Sound of E	34
V	The Short Vowel Sound of I	101
VI	The Short Vowel Sound of I	69
VII	The Long Vowel Sound of O	125
VIII	The Short Vowel Sound of O	35
IX	The Long Vowel Sound of U	11
X	The Short Vowel Sound of U	38
XI	The Long Diphthong Sound of OO (boot)	82
XII	The Short Diphthong Sound of OO (look)	2
XIII	The Diphthong Sound of AU (haul, taught)	27
XIV	The Diphthong Sound of OI (boil, oil)	5
XV	The Diphthong Sound of OU (foul, out)	13
XVI	The r-Controlled Sound of AR (far)	17
XVIIA	The r-Controlled Sound of OR (for)	51

XVIIB The r-Controlled Sound
of **OR** (world)   4

XVIII The r-Controlled Sound
of **ER** (her, tern)   16

XIX The r-Controlled Sound
of **IR** (fir, sir)   10

XX The r-Controlled Sound
of **UR** (fur, hurt)   15

    Simple Homonyn Count - 1046
    Complex Homonym Count - 269

    Total Homonym Count - 1315

Appendix D

Definitions and Abbreviations

A - Definitions

Affix - an affix is a word element, a prefix or a suffix, which is attached before or after a root. These elements affect meaning significantly, as in *repeat, discover, inaction, progressive,* etc. (See Inflection)

Archaic - designates words and language that were once common but are now used chiefly to suggest an earlier style or period.

British - of, pertaining to, or characteristic of, Great Britain, the United Kingdom, or the British Empire.

Complex Root - a root which involves a complex interaction involving a simple base root which has been enlarged, or incremented, by prefixes, suffixes, and/or inflections. The addition of these affixes significantly influences the semantic value of the base root in ways very different than that which occurs when a simple root is enlarged by the addition of an inflection, a change which affects tense, person, number, gender, etc :
  Simple Root plus inflections - *late-later-latest*
  Complex Root plus affixes - *relate-relation-relativity*

Defining sentence - one which presents significant information about word meaning within the context provided by the sentence itself.

Diphthong - a complex speech sound consisting of two vowels pronounced as a single syllable, as in *oi-oy, ou-ow,* etc.

Homonym - a homonym is a word which agrees with another in pronunciation, but differs from it in meaning, origin, and spelling.

Inflection - an ending attached to a root which affects person, number, tense, gender, etc.,but which does not significantly affect root meaning, as in *jump, jumps, jumping, jumped, jumper, jumpy, etc.*

Informal - language which is considered part of natural spoken language, but inappropriate in some cultural contexts, as in standard written prose of ceremonial or official communications.

Law - used to indicate that a word is one relating to language used specifically in legal matters.

Nonstandard - used to designate words which do not belong to any standard, educated speech, and also for words which have come into being through error, such as *ain't.*

Obsolete - indicates that a word is no longer in use.

Poetic - having a quality or style characteristic of poetry.

r-Controlled Sound - indicates a vowel whose pronunciation is significantly influenced by the presence of a following consonant **r**, as in *ar-er-ir-or-ur*

Rare - occurring infrequently or uncommon.

Regional - a word little used in only a particular section or area.

Root Vowel - indicates an individual vowel element which serves as the essential unifying element in a word or root. Such a vowel may stand alone, as in *a-e-i-o-r,* or in direct sequence with another vowel, as in *ee-ie-oa-oo-oi,* or with its *signal e,* as in *a-e, e-e, i-e, o-e, u-e.*

Scottish - of, pertaining to, or characteristic of, Scotland or its people.

Simple Root (also Simple Base Root) - a root that contains tains a single vowel element and one or more consonants in its *basic* form, and is *simple*, in that it functions independently and in the absence of inflections and/or affixes, as in *deep, storm, black, loud, etc.*

Slang - nonstandard vocabulary of a given culture or subculture.

Vulgar - indicates that the word is not simply *slang*, but rather that there is a social taboo attached to a particular word.

B - Abbreviations

adj	- adjective
adv	- adverb
conj	- conjunction
contr	- contraction
inf	- infinitive
interj	- interjection
n	- noun
pro	- pronoun
prep	- preposition
v	- verb

Bibliography
1. *Websters New Twentieth Century Dictionary of the English Language* (Second Edition). Collins World, New York, NY. 1978
2. *The American Heritage Dictionary of the English Language.* Houghton Mifflin, Boston, MA. 1973
3. *Britannica World Language Dictionary.* Funk & Wagnalls, New York, NY. 1959
4. *The Compact Edition of the Oxford Englsh Language Dictionary.* Oxford University Press, Oxford, England. 1971
5. *The Oxford Dictionary of English Etymology.* Clarendon Press, London, Enbland. 1966
6. Laurita, R.E. *The New Spelling - Orthographic Structur-alism.* Leonardo Press, Camden, ME. 1981
7. Laurita, R.E. *The Vowel Category Resource Lists - Part One and Part Two.* Leonardo Press, Camden, ME. (1980-(1981)
8. Laurita, R.E. *Greek Roots and their Modern English Spellings.* Leonardo Press, Camden, ME. 1989